Human Resource Development in
EDUCATION

To order additional copies of this book, contact
Partridge India
000 800 10062 62
orders.india@partridgepublishing.com

www.partridgepublishing.com/india

Human Resource Development in
EDUCATION

By
DR. K.S. BHARDWAJ

Chief Executive Officer,
Shri Ram Ahuja Group of Educational Institutions,
Shikohabad, Distt. Firozabad (UP) India

2014

PARTRIDGE
A Penguin Random House Company

CONTENTS

Chapter 1

Performance Appraisal: Present Scenario 1

1.1   The Present Scenario: 1
1.2   Importance of Performance Appraisal 3
1.3   Definition of Performance Appraisal......................................6
1.4   Performance Appraisal in Education 7
1.5   Objectives of Teachers' Appraisal:..9
1.6   Characteristics of Appraisal Procedure................................10
1.7   Prerequisites of Performance Appraisal: 12
1.8   Preparation for Successful Performance Appraisal:............14
1.9   Who Should Appraise the Teachers?.....................................15

Chapter 2

Performance Appraisal in Education: Special Discussion 20

2.1   Difference between Industrial Performance Appraisal
        and Educational one..20
2.2   Principles of Educational Performance Appraisal:.............22
2.3   Cycle/Procedure of Performance Appraisal........................25
2.4   Self-appraisal:..28
2.5   Logic behind Self-appraisal:..28
2.6   Procedure of Self-appraisal 31
2.7   Role-Play: A Note 33
2.8   Qualities of Role-play:..34
2.9   Features of Role-playing:..34

Chapter 3

Performance Appraisal: Guidelines 36

3.1   Philosophy of Performance appraisal:...................................36
3.2   Desired Objectives of Performance
        Appraisal Philosophy: 37
3.3   Accountability of the Organisation:.......................................38
3.4   Formal Performance Appraisal: 39
3.5   Procedure of Annual Performance Appraisal Review:........39
3.6   Performance Improvement: 41
3.7   Logic behind Performance Appraisal:....................................42

3.8   Policy Statement: 43

3.9   Appraisal: Modus Operandy: 43

3.10   Rapport and Appraisal: 44

3.11   The Culture of Voluntary Co-operation: Characteristics:....47

3.12   Characteristics of Forced Culture: 49

Chapter 4

Managerial Vision of Teachers' Performance Appraisal.....................52

4.1   Performance Review: 53

4.2   Staff Development Review: 53

4.3   Individual and Organisational Needs: 54

4.4   Organisational Management Styles: 57

4.5   Organisational Scenario and Appraisal: 59

4.6   Appraisal Process: Its Limitations: 61

4.7   The Appraisal Potentialities: 62

4.8   Kinds of Staff-Appraisal: 63

4.9   Perspectives of Appraisal in Teaching: 67

Chapter 5

Teachers' Appraisal Procedures 72

5.1   Analytical Review of Self-appraisal: 72

5.2   Prior Steps for Self appraisal: 73

5.3   Students for Feedback on Teaching: 74

5.4   Significance of Students' Feedback: 75

5.5   Forms of Teachers' Appraisal: 76

5.6   Accountability Centric Appraisal: 76

5.7   Professional Centric Appraisal: 78

5.8   Employee Centric Appraisal: 80

5.9   Critical Analysis of Performance Appraisal Practices: 80

5.10   Diagnosis of Appraisal Errors: 86

5.11   Conclusion: 87

Chapter 6

Need-based Performance Appraisal 89

6.1   Goals of Need-based Performance Appraisal: 91

6.2   Managerial Goals: 91

6.3   Performance-Appraisal Goals: 91

6.4   General Goals: 91

6.5   Need-based Appraisal Procedures: 92

6.6	Principles of Appraisal:	93
6.7	Selection of Appraisers:	94
6.8	Appraisal Preparations:	94
6.9	Appraisal Interviews:	96
6.10	Appraisal Report:	98
6.11	Complaints Redressal Procedures:	99
6.12	Follow-up Actions:	99
6.13	More Follow-up-actions:	101
6.14	More Suggestions	101

Chapter 7
Appraisal Discussion: Necessary Skills 103
7.1	Stimulants for Appraisal Discussion/Interviews:	103
7.2	Face-to-Face Process: Main Features of.	105
7.3	Main Skills of Appraisal Discussion:	106
7.4	Pre-discussion Skills:	107
7.5	Main Discussion Skills:	107
7.6	Post-discussion Skills:	108

Chapter 8
Bottlenecks in Teachers' Performance Appraisal 109
8.1	Obstacles in Effective Appraisal in Education:	110
8.2	Some Developments Influencing Performance Appraisal of Teachers:	116
8.3	Performance Appraisal Systems:	120

Chapter 9
Human Resource Development, Appraisals and Rewards 122
9.1	Development of Personnel:	122
9.2	Senior Subordinates' Appraisal:	126
9.3	Procedure of Performance Appraisal:	127
9.4	Advantages of Performance Appraisal:	137
9.5	Good Performance Rewards:	140

Chapter 10
Managements' Awakening 142
10.1	Fixing of Goals and Performance Standards:	147
10.2	Performance Appraisal: The Logic:	148
10.3	Managerial Roles in Performance Appraisal:	148

10.4   Teachers' Responsibilities: 149
10.5   Duties of Human Resource Department:.............................150
10.6   Pre-appraisal Discussion: 150
10.7   Duties of the Appraiser:..151
10.8   Precautions in Preparing the Appraisal-Plan:....................152
10.9   Contemplations on Appraisal:...153
10.10   Characteristics of Effective Appraisal: 154
10.11   Providing Feedback:..155

Chapter 11
Continuous Performance Monitoring..158
11.1   Advantages and Disadvantages of Continuous
        Performance Monitoring: 159
11.2   Problem Solving during Continuous Performance
        Monitoring:...160
11.3   Conclusion: 165

Chapter 12
Performance Appraisal Forms 169
12.1   Suggestions regarding Appraisal:..170
12.2   Performance Appraisal Proformas: 171

Subject wise Index
Appraisal..193

ABOUT THE BOOK

Human Resource Development in Education is that treatise which will be useful not only for the Managers, Principals and Appraisers but also benefit the teachers by making them aware of their pious duties towards the students and their parents' expectations in particular and the entire society in general. This book highlights the significance of providing in-service opportunities for higher education to the teachers and paving effective ways to appraise their efficiency and proficiency thereafter; and making further arrangements for their need-based in-service or on-job training if need be for their professional development. It will enlighten the Educational Managers and Administrators to the extent what assignment ought to be given to which teacher for the smooth functioning of the institution so that wastage in terms of time, money and manpower could be reduced to a great extent. It further highlights the importance of timely "feedback" for the teacher from appraiser and for the students from the teachers. The appraisers have been cautioned against the futility of appraisal sans quick "feedback" to the appraisees.

This book studies the positive results and significance of effective leadership, well-spelled objectives of educational management, effects of voluntary collaborative work-culture, role-playing qualities of student friendly teachers and their capabilities for self-appraisal threadbare and further guides the teachers effectively. The writer has been a successful teacher and educational-administrator. His experiences have enriched this book and they make its study educative and interesting; prompting the teachers to revisit their methods of teaching and providing in-time feedback to the students.

We feel this book will prove to be a milestone in the management of education. But we do not claim it to be a final word. We shall hail a thorough appraisal of this work. Hence suggestions from the academicians are welcome at jainarayangaur@yahoo.com

ABOUT THE AUTHOR

Dr. K.S. Bhardwaj is a Ph.D. in Education, Post-graduate in English, Sociology and Education, Post-graduate Diploma in the Teaching of English and Post-graduate Diploma in Training and Development. He has been Director-Principal of several Teachers' Training Colleges in India. Presently he is the Chief Executive Officer with Shri Ram Ahuja Group of Educational Institutions at Shikohabad, Distt. Firozabad, UP, India. He has been the Vice-President of the Council of Teacher Education (Haryana Chapter). He has authored and published 'Humour in Classroom', 'Microteaching: Theory and Practice', 'Shikshan-kshetriya Manav Sansadhan Vikas' 'Teaching of Social Sciences' with Prof. Ruhela and 'Essentials of Microteaching' with Prof. A. Rambabu. Second revised edition of 'Humour in Classroom' coming soon. He has authored literary works too like 'Shashwat Prem' (Hindi fiction dealing with sex-psychology of women) and 'Samay ke Hastakshar' (An anthology of Hindi poems). His stories 'The Farewell' and 'The Albatross' appeared in Kashmiri English journal Miras. His paper 'Challenges in Teacher education in Present Scenario with reference to Pupil-Teacher' appeared in CTE Journal (UP-Chapter) 2007 and a research paper on 'Germane Humour' in Educational Review published by NCERT, Delhi. Articles in Hindi and English appeared in various journals/magazines from time to time.

Some unpublished works are: Nursery Education in India, Academic Management Development, Orchard in the Backyard (English fiction on women's psyche about men), Eternal Love (English novel on women's sex-psychology), The Leech (English novel on women's sex-exploitation), and 'Could Akbar be Great Without Birbal?' (An analytical historical review of Mughal Emperor Akbar) etc.

FOREWORD

Most of the educational institutions are very well aware of the successful experiments their teachers have made and teaching techniques that they use quite often because this process through which they know all this, is the part of the performance appraisal. It appraises their work-skills, takes note of their achievements in the light of standards of qualitative improvement and judges the developmental policies of the organisation which facilitate the smooth functioning of the employees leading to a cohesive environment in it. Even then performance appraisal depends on several factors. It is important for any organisation that it keeps new plans ready suitable to the skills and capabilities of its employees. This is as important as the holistic approach to any issue. Performance appraisal starts right from the interview/interaction between an employee and the management at the time of his/her selection and passes through his/her individual performance development through in-service training leading to his/her holistic development. This way the performance appraisal is actually the foundation of human resource development.

It will be our first step towards success if we can make the performance-appraisal-training-curriculum acceptable to all the concerned because it will establish a balance between performance appraisal process and training and development process thus strengthening both.

The writer's personal experience is whenever performance-appraisal was made development oriented and whenever all the stake-holders (teachers, students, parents and others) were given equal or desired importance in this process; then not only the results were found to be very good and encouraging but improved the total educational scenario also. Not only the teachers but the students and parents satisfaction was more than it was expected. The students self-confidence increased, students-teachers day to day interaction improved and the education process became more effective.

One thing I want to make explicitly clear. It is often feared if students are more involved in the performance appraisal of teachers then they will become more disrespectful to them. Our experiences in this regard are different. It is well-known that the students still have more firm faith in their teachers than their parents. This firm faith gets shattered only when they find teachers behaving against that model image which they had formed in their minds. What are those standards which the students hold about their teachers? These are good character, helpful, sensitive to students' needs, expert in their teaching subjects and student-loving. In other words we can say that the students see their role-models in their teachers. When this image of teachers gets demolished, the students vision gets blurred and start ignoring their teachers and showing disrespect to them. The teachers, who take care to maintain the above qualities, are always instinctively respected by their students. They are always dear to their students. Another example is that the low-esteemed teachers are given funny names by their students but those with a high-esteem are never given names; and if given those too match their good qualities. Whether the students are entrusted with this appraisal work or not even then they continue with the informal appraisal of their teachers.

Continuity and creativity is essential for the educational development process. But it is possible only in a cordial atmosphere of mutual trust and mutual respect. Healthy academic environment is not possible without the cooperation of educational administrators, parents, society and the community. Education delivery process has to be development oriented to meet the educational needs of the students. I have prepared this book with this view. In the fast changing world, Self-appraisal and Students' Feedback are highly significant which the teachers ought to pay special attention to. Hence the former has been mainly highlighted twice in Chapters two and five. Moreover this treatise too may not be a final word. Therefore suggestions of the practicing academicians are always welcome at jainarayangaur@ yahoo.com or by post at the address given below. Thanks for patient reading.

dr. bhardwaj, k.s.   Basant Panchami
Flat No. 95-A, Sector D,
Pocket 2 Kondli Gharoli Complex,
Mayur Vihar 3 New Delhi 110096   **jainarayangaur@yahoo.com**

FOREWORD

Human Resource Development in Education is an important area but most of the teacher educators and practicing schoolteachers and educational authorities at least in India do not know exactly what it is and how is of relevance to them. There are no books available on this crucial theme. I am happy to find that Dr.K.S.Bhardwaj, a very experienced educationist, who has a long and rich practical experience of teaching in and administering a number of senior secondary schools and teachers colleges and has been a close participant observer of how teachers' performance is usually evaluated in a slipshod manner in our country, has come out with this important and highly instructive book on this crucial aspect of educational institutions.

All educationists, educational authorities and our leaders in our culture and society have usually been talking of the high place and importance of teachers' role functioning in platitudes, but very few of them really know how much tension-ridden, confused and dissatisfied most of school teachers and teacher educators really are mainly because they find that neither there are well laid down proper and practicable policies and procedures which they are supposed to follow, nor most of the teachers know that their role functioning is usually not properly and judiciously evaluated by the educational authorities — those who work sincerely and properly and those who do not do so are usually treated with the same yardstick and when the time of recommending or nominating most efficient teacher/s for state level and national level annual awards and honor to them comes, usually it is seen that the sincere, conscientious and efficient teachers and teacher-educators are invariably sidelined by most of the heads of the institution, and usually the flatterers, teacher politicians or satellites of local, state level or national level influential politician leaders are selected for these awards. This has been my experience as a sociologist of education in India for the last five decades. Most teachers have lost any fascination, enthusiasm and the very faith in the Annual Teacher's awards due to this pungent sociological truth of our democratic nation. The same story is being repeated year after year.

Dr. Bhardwaj's book strongly emphasizes that teachers' performance appraisal must be done properly. It should be morale-boosting, job related, objective, continuous and two-way profession-centric, need-based, face to face procedure according to sound principles.

It is an excellent and much needed academic contribution which shall be welcomed by all those who are involved in the ongoing educational revolution in the 21st century India and really clamor for fair and humane play in the teaching profession. This book shall be of great value and use a guide book to all educators and educational administrators in Indus and all developing and modernizing nations.

Dr. Bhardwaj has been my earliest Ph.D. scholar in Education in the Jamia Millia Islamia, New Delhi in the 1970s. The topic of his doctoral research was 'Humor in Classroom'. Therefore, I was expecting that he would be including some humorous incidents, jokes, cartoons to make his serious book on 'Human Resource Development in Education' very interesting and eye-catching for all its readers. I have seen a number of humorous jokes about teachers in humor books and humorous cartoon in a foreign journal of Educational Technology and Delhi Government Education guidebook on Adolescence Education some years Back. So why they can't be here in this book? Some of them could and should have found their legitimate place in this serious book to become joyful and useful. May be, he may like to devote a few pages in this book in its further editions.

April 25, 2014   Dr. Satya Pal Ruhela
Retired Professor of Education(Sociology),
Head of Teacher Training Department, Dean
of Faculty of Education, & Offg. V.C.,
Jamia Millia Islamis (Central University),
New Delhi-110025.
E-Mail:spruhela@gmail.com

DEDICATED TO

My father Swargeey Pandit Singh Ramji
A dynamic and innovative Headmaster of his times
My mother Smt Bharti, and all those especially
Professor S.P. Ruhela who guided me
And shaped my personality
<u>From time to time.</u>

CHAPTER 1

Performance Appraisal: Present Scenario

1.1 The Present Scenario:

In educational institutions, evaluation of teaching is not new. It has been in practice in one form or the other for long. The teachers' diary whether it is daily or weekly and its presentation before the Principal and his comments thereupon to back up the teacher on his good work or to improve further are the forms of performance appraisal which continues unabatedly in the schools. The Principal makes his notes in respect of each teacher on the basis of these diaries/classroom inspections and uses them for the betterment of the institution and the particular teacher. The traditional confidential reports filed by him annually in respect of each teacher are another form of annual performance appraisal. The teachers' annual increments, efficiency bars and further promotions or demotions in case of gross negligence by any teacher, are given on the basis of these confidential reports popularly known as CRs. The teachers are very well aware that their teaching work, general conduct and teaching expertise are being regularly monitored and evaluated by the Principals, higher educational authorities, parents, teachers and the public in general through these formal and informal techniques which may be unscientific and haphazard on account of the their subjectivity. Biannual departmental inspections of schools too are part of such performance appraisals. But these performance appraisals have been mostly negative as they focus on finding faults with the teachers. These have been seldom developmental, reformatory or counseling. Most of the time, the minor weaknesses or faults of the teachers are kept confidential and never told to them curtailing all possible chances to correct them and improve. And if ever conveyed in case of gross violations, these are given in writing which annoy the teachers more than showing them any way to improve. Such confidential reports are more condemnatory than reforming. The concerned

1

teacher feels being let down. It reduces all chances for him to see the reason of the criticism and improve.

But the fast changing scenario from authoritarian to democratic has necessitated for the appraisers to change their attitudes, modify the techniques of appraisals to make them more scientific, trustworthy dependable, organised and progressive. But such processes are still in progress.

Besides the above mentioned techniques of appraisal, other methods being used by the schools and colleges for this purpose are not uniform. Not only this, they are unreliable because of their subjectivity and lack of objectivity. That is why such confidential reports or appraisal methods are looked down upon by the teachers and are quite often challenged. Instead of making any improvements, such confidential reports spoil cordial relations between the teachers and the principal resulting in hostile atmosphere in the institutions which could never be conducive to academic growth and educational development. Its brunt has to be borne by the students in particular and the parents in general.

Actually it seems as if the traditional appraisal system of confidential reports (CRs) was just to keep an effective control over the staff/teachers. It, instead of being progressive was actually regressive as it humiliated the workers/teachers more than showing them a way to improve. Confidential reports (CRs) never accounted for the good qualities of the teachers. On the other hand, they centered on their mistakes and only those were brought to their notice which was necessary. The good qualities seldom found place in these reports. Since these reports took cognizance only of the personality traits, the teacher/worker felt discouraged and often stopped taking interest in his work. Appraisal should be of the work not of the personality so as to show a way to improve the working-skills. The name of this system "confidential reports" itself indicates secrecy which filled the work place with negativity badly affecting the working skills. Instead of developing cordiality among teachers/workers and the management, it introduced hostility against each other. Teaching is no less than a "performing art" which could fine tune and survive only in an environment of understanding.

This type of subjective and unrealistic approach was never welcome by the teachers. They hated the very idea of internal inspection by the principal or external inspection by the department because they carried out these appraisals according to their whims and fancies; and focused on the teachers' weaknesses. Since these appraisals created a sense of guilt among the teachers, they could never win their hearts. Disagreement among teachers and appraisers/management surfaced. After such biased appraisal they rather became more aggressive and hostile to the authorities. Sometimes, the relations among them became so strained that they led to protests and strikes; and sometimes reached courts too. By such approaches, what the management could gain is beyond comprehension.

This form of appraisal being one sided is considered by the teachers just as a weapon in the hands of the management to harm them. Such a scenario curtails healthy professional and institutional development. It blocks individual growth and brings a bad name to the management/institution. But of late, the things are now slowly changing.

1.2 Importance of Performance Appraisal

Performance appraisal is that process which appraises the professional conduct and work skills of an employee/teacher during a certain period. Its main objective is to assess the utility of an employee/teacher for the organisation. Thus performance appraisal is that organised practice which judges the skills of a teacher to complete the tasks entrusted to him by his organisation. It helps in identifying those teachers who can or cannot accomplish a particular job skillfully in a given time; and if they cannot, what specific reasons are thereof and what and how the organisation could do to remove those difficulties in the successful completion of the job. It is thus a joint exercise to identify the potential of the teachers on one hand and the organisational potentials for the teachers' professional growth, secure their future, give job-satisfaction to the teachers and document the achievements of the teachers on the other so as to:

- Appraise the teachers' teaching skills objectively.
- Ensure smooth and effective functioning of the institution.

- Ensure professional growth of the teachers.
- Secure the future of the teachers.
- Train the teachers in self-appraisal.
- Highlight the organisational goals.
- Finalize the strategies to implement the policies of the educational institutions with the mutual consent of teachers and the management.
- Reward good performance, help the under-achievers to improve and relieve the non-performers.

Needless to say that teacher performance appraisal system could be effectively implemented only when the teachers are well trained in self-appraisal. It may look difficult but not at all impossible. It is universally accepted that self-detected errors in working could be easily, readily and effectively rectified by the doer than after being pointed out by others. Self-appraisal requires detection of own faults which is indeed very difficult because pointing fingers on others is rather easy than pointing a finger on self. It can be done only by self-actualizing teachers who are honest to themselves, sincere in realizing own mistakes, have the will to rectify them and feel accountable to their work and duties.

There are two main advantages of performance appraisal:

➤ Administrative: Information collected through performance appraisal is used to: —

- Promote, transfer or depute any teacher to another place.
- Demote, remove, dismiss or layoff.
- Increase in salary, sanction bonus and reward good performance.

➤ Developmental Feedback: Data collected through performance appraisal is used for the following purposes also.

- To strengthen the teachers' teaching skills.
- Weaknesses of the teachers are put before them and motivated to overcome them.
- And the ways to improve are suggested.

A cursory look at the above mentioned goals of performance appraisal system indicates that this ought to be fully objective. The more objective it is, the more effective it will be. That is why the managers of education have started replacing confidential reports by other modern appraisal techniques and methods. These appraisal techniques and methods are being effectively used in industry for long and these have earned the trust of the managements as well as the workers. These techniques and methods are more transparent, flexible, give more say to the workers and promote participative management. These appraisal methods and techniques focus on what, how and when a worker performs well instead of focusing on his personal traits. It considerably reduces the chances of the appraiser to be subjective, using his likes and dislikes and appraising the workers on the basis of his whims and fancies. The modern appraisal techniques are used to develop the performance skills of the workers which lead to his personal growth too; advantages of which ultimately reach the organisation. It is not only a measuring tool of his performance but it is also for his professional and personal growth. Thus appraisal is a qualitative perennial process of individual and organisational growth and development.

Performance appraisal can therefore be termed as quality-gauzing tool. Pre-determined set of goals and achievements are set aside. They may be used as motivators but not as testing scales. The appraiser's beliefs do not have any place in modern appraisal techniques. Workers' working styles and skills are important and these need to be appraised. Appraiser's likes and dislikes of the appraisee have no place in the modern techniques of appraisal. Instead, focusing on the work-skills of the workers, the appraisal system aims at providing meaningful feedback to the concerned worker so that a good performer could improve further and an average-performer avails himself of the suggestions, guidance and advice of the appraiser to improve his skills. Modern appraisal techniques thus centre on quality of performance than on the personal characteristics of the workers. And the feedback is also given keeping these objectives in mind. It is the charisma of this type of the feedback that the workers improve their work styles, hone up their skills and not only self-develop but also contribute significantly in organisational growth and development. Modern appraisal system being positive brims with cooperation, coordination and mutual understanding. And it is not a stopgap practice. It is rather never-ending which starts from the entry level of a teacher in the institution and goes up to his leaving it: Optimistically going beyond that too as the teacher is sure to use those earlier learnt skills in some other institution. It will not be an exaggeration if it is called **PERRENIAL.** A healthy performance appraisal system can be effectively used to train the teachers according to the work-culture of the educational institution/organisation and their teaching skills can be tuned fast to the needs of time, place and prevailing circumstances.

An ideal performance appraisal yields mainly three positive results: One, judging the teaching skills of a teacher in an objective manner and preparing records which could be used for the development of the organisation/institution. Second, development of teaching skills of a teacher and if any need for improvement is needed, rendering a sympathetic counselling and back-up to do so. Third, it appraises the facilities available in the institution which improve or block up good performance of the teachers. The main point of success in this process is how much positive and objective the appraiser is. The more objective, impartial and teaching-related performance appraisal is the better chances of institutional as well as individual development are.

1.3   Definition of Performance Appraisal

Performance appraisal means judging the work skills of a worker, using his skills for the institutional/organisational growth, analyse his interests in the organisation and find/suggest ways and means to enhance his interests if required. Please note that it aims at the development of the individual more than the organisation because if the workers' skills are better and his interests in the organisation increase, the ultimate beneficiary will certainly be the organisation. So a wise performance appraiser will focus on the individual's growth and development instead of the organisation. It is like tending the roots of a tree. If the roots are healthy, tree itself will remain fresh and green and brim with life. On the contrary, if the roots get dried or rotten, the tree can never survive. There is no possibility of it.

Evaluation and appraisal are quite often considered synonymous in management literature. But both are quite different. "Appraisal" is preferred than "evaluation" in modern performance appraisal philosophy. In 1944, Robert Pace and Maurice Troyer had said, "What is evaluation in education? It is the process of judging the effectiveness of educational experience." Today the appraiser substitutes "evaluation" with "appraisal." Actually this confusion is because "appraisal" is a member of the word-family which consists of evaluation, assessment, monitoring, reviewing, estimation, gauging, judging etc. In contrast to other words of this family, "appraise" is peculiar as it indicates a continuity of this process. Except in appraisal, marking system is extensively used in evaluation, assessment, and estimation or gauging. In this sense, reviewing and monitoring are more close to appraisal. But they too fall short of appraisal. Though "marking-system" when needed, is used to some extent by appraisers also but it being against the philosophy of appraisal is quite often frowned upon by the modern management experts. Appraisal is not only judging the work-skills of a teacher but also consists of providing feedback for professional growth, need-based counselling, facilities and environment conducive to individual and organisational development and help to overcome the difficulties coming in the way of improvement or smooth functioning. So it is more than giving marks or grades to any teacher. In other words, appraisal is more diagnostic and reformative. It also acknowledges the plus points of a teacher which encourages him to work more diligently and earn more praise in future. Thus the appraisal system is more positive. Negativity has no place in this system. Its fruits are equally relished by teachers and managers/appraisers. It is norm based.

1.4   Performance Appraisal in Education

Educational institutions are set up with specific objectives and sincere efforts are made to realise them. One of the principal duties of the management is to ensure that its set objectives are really being achieved or not. All the resources put at the disposal of the teachers to realise those objectives, are being utilized optimally or not. And for this, the managements need to appraise the teachers as well as the available resources including tools and environment in the institution.

When we think of appraisal in education, the first and foremost idea of appraising anyone rests on the teacher and his teaching skills as he is the pivot of the whole teaching system. And the teacher's success depends on his communication capabilities, expression skills, clarity of concepts and their clear and effective presentation; will to update his knowledge, his conduct in the class and his desire to be a model teacher. So his appraisal in education also focuses on his professional growth and its continuous further appraisal.

Therefore, it is incumbent upon the education managers to frame a scientific and objective appraisal scheme before planning educational projects and implementing them. Launching educational projects without proper appraisal system will be a futile attempt as they are likely to fall short of the set goals because the developmental process and performance appraisal go hand in hand. Both are inter-related. Existence of one is impossible without the other. As said earlier, the main objective of appraisal is to speed up the process of professional growth of the teachers and development of the organisation. It therefore, can never be of any use in establishing supremacy over the teachers and discipline them in a traditional way. Appraisals in education ought to be looked at as tools to improve the quality of teaching. Taking note of the success of teachers, it should prepare such data which account for the growth of teachers as well as the institution. Appraisal in education is three-pronged:

➢ To bring the teachers face to face with their weaknesses and assist them to overcome them.
➢ To help the teachers in identifying their individual goals with those of the institution.
➢ To assess the institutional infrastructure available to the teachers necessary for performance.

The main basis for the above rests on the following:

• Assessment of the teacher's interests and his inclinations towards his institution and its use for it.
• Compare the working-skills of the teacher with the set-goals.
• Bring them into the knowledge of the teacher.

- Provide the low achiever proper guidance to improve and an opportunity to him he does so.
- Provide necessary ways and means for improvement including environment conducive to reforms and other necessary equipment/tools etc.

1.5   Objectives of Teachers' Appraisal:

We may categorize them in two parts: (A) Evaluative (B) Developmental. The former is used to fix salaries, give increments, promotions, lay-offs and to take other administrative decisions. The latter focus on engaging teachers in research, providing feedback on their teaching performance, plan the manpower, improve performance and establish a rapport between the teachers and the management. For this, performance appraisal process needs to be most transparent, suitably flexible, reliable and designed and implemented with the mutual consent of the management and the teachers. The following steps can help in fulfilling the above conditions:

- Managerial Development: For this such managerial philosophy is adopted which supports transparency in management and prepares the teachers keeping future needs in mind and in such a way that they (teachers) bear their increased responsibilities easily and happily. In this process the teachers' consent is also taken. In other words, all decisions are taken collectively which take care of individual and organisation needs equally.
- Performance scale: Objectivity based performance scale is finalised. It is that scale which gauges teachers' teaching skills according to institutional goals.
- Salary and other benefits: On the basis of objective appraisal teachers' salaries and bonus is settled in a transparent manner. Being transparent, it wins the confidence of teachers as well.
- Skills identification: Objective appraisal easily identifies teachers' teaching skills and work is allotted according to their capacity. It benefits the institution as well as the teacher as it opens channels for the teachers' promotions etc. Positive part of this approach is that the teachers take deep interest in all the institutional activities and it leads to his development. Contrary

to it if we assign any job or work and give the teacher or worker the tools against his interests and capacity then the results will be similar to those that we will have to face by giving a razor to a simian. He will either injure himself or us. Higher chances are that he will harm us. So this much precaution is necessary for the managements to see what job and tool is given to whom. It will be more in its favour than anyone else.

- Feedback: Objective appraisal identifies the weaknesses of the teacher with a sympathetic look and brings them to his notice suggesting ways to overcome them. Feedback is also used to spell out the organisational goals and to make them explicitly clear before the teachers. When the individual or organisational expectations are clear, performance will be better and organisations will be more sensitive to the individual needs.

- Manpower planning: Objective appraisals help the managers to estimate the manpower needs of the institution and make it available, make the best use of the available talent, guide and improve the average performers and get rid of non-performers. The last step if taken in any case ought to be taken in consultation with other prominent faculty members so as to root out any possibility of discontentment later.

- Rapport between the teachers and the management: Objective appraisals do a great job of establishing communication channels between the teachers and the management. For this, a pro forma is prepared highlighting individual and institutional goals by mutual understanding. It develops trust between seniors and juniors. Clarity of goals leads to making functional strategies at each level and a healthy work-culture. Cordial atmosphere is created at the workplace. Naturally, it leads to better performance at every level and good output is ensured. Other objectives of appraisal could be: Research, demotions, removals, dismissals, recruitments etc.

1.6   Characteristics of Appraisal Procedure

Characteristics of appraisal system are as follows:

- ➢ Performance expectation must be clear. Until the teachers know what they are expected to do and what for, they cannot perform well. The teachers should not be left groping in the dark. Clarity of purpose is a must for success.

➢ Balance between individual and institutional/organisational goals must be established fast. Opposition between the two will be detrimental to smooth functioning of institution, cordial relations between managers and teachers and peaceful environment at the workplace.

➢ Ideal appraisal system is based on mutual understanding. It must be designed through mutual discussion. It will develop a work-culture based on cooperation and coordination.

➢ Appraisal ought to be done by trained and experienced experts. Appraisal by untrained and inexperienced appraisers will never win the confidence of appraisee. In my long teaching career, only one appraiser had come who had won my trust with his expertise and role-modeling and I had learnt a lot from him.

➢ Appraisal system ought to be morale boosting. At least it should never be leg-pulling. It should not be directly linked to rise in salaries or promotions but may be used indirectly to encourage good performers.

➢ Appraisal should be absolutely work related and should not have anything to do with the personal traits of the appraisee. It should be discreet, rational and logical.

➢ Management has every right to reward anyone or not to. But undue delay in rewarding good performers must be avoided. It harms more than rewarding late.

➢ The appraisal must be made on the basis of standard principles. It must recognize the good performance immediately and instead of condemning or punishing the poor performers, they should be properly guided to improve.

➢ Appraisal is a continuing process guided by well defined principles, leading to follow-up-action so that complaint redressal could be addressed to. Continuity is its chief characteristic.

➢ An ideal appraisal scheme ought to be transparent and is open to appraisees. There should not be any secrecy until very necessary.

➢ The results of an ideal appraisal scheme based on scientific approach ought to be fully utilized to achieve individual as well as organisational goals.

> ➤ During the teachers' appraisal, only the measureable areas like home work, class work, probing questions, attention-seeking questions etc. ought to be included in it and quantified.
> ➤ All organisations must have a grievance redressal system and it ought to be swift and based on objective decision making process.

There is no doubt that implementation of ideal performance appraisal scheme is not a child's play as it faces a lot of difficulties and obstacles but the enlightened managements always brace up to face them and implement such performance appraisal schemes which are beneficial not only for the organisations but teachers/workers as well and are helpful in implementation of all-friendly and useful projects. It is certain that the performance appraisal schemes which are bereft of the above characteristics can never establish a rapport between the managements and teachers/workers. Such performance appraisal schemes will rather create differences among them. Such an environment full of negativity can never be conducive to development either for the organisation or its members.

1.7 Prerequisites of Performance Appraisal:

The success of performance appraisal scheme does not depend only on its right implementation but it also requires a few prerequisites as well for it otherwise the whole process may become defunct. These prerequisites are: —

> ➤ Management's deep faith, commitment and attachment with the performance appraisal scheme are very essential. The more the management is committed to the appraisal scheme, the more successful it will be. The managers will have to shed off their negativity towards the teachers and render their full support to such appraisal schemes which are useful for teachers as well as the institution.
> ➤ Performance appraisal scheme ought to be fit for achieving the individual and institutional goals.
> ➤ Performance appraisal scheme should fit in the work-culture and the means of the institution. Whatever funds and infrastructure is needed for the successful implementation of the appraisal scheme must be prearranged.

> Teachers too must have full faith in the appraisal scheme. They should feel assured that the scheme is for their benefit and not against them.
> Performance appraisal scheme ought to be designed with the consents and cooperation of the teachers so that they have full faith in the scheme as well as the appraisers/management.
> Appraisal scale should also be trustworthy and be able to win the trust of the appraisees.
> The appraisees should also feel assured that there will be no interference of the management in the objective appraisal.

If the organisations/institutions desire that the appraisal system develops on healthy and modern thinking, then above prerequisites should also be fulfilled. It is pertinent to point out here that the appraisal system is two-pronged and all from top to bottom join and participate in it. Its success depends on the active participation of both. If it does not happen due to one reason or the other, it is the duty of the management to ensure participation of all because they are the policy makers and trend-setters. They head the organisation and are empowered to make any changes in the existing policies or making new ones suitable to changing times and trends. Thus the onus of successful performance appraisal lies only on the management.

Another moot point is that who will appraise the appraisers. Teachers' little doubt or no faith on their superiors' capabilities or impartiality will kill the purpose of appraisal. Unflinching faith of the teachers in their appraisers is their biggest asset and if it is shaken, its restoration becomes very difficult until they start getting appraised by their subordinates: May be voluntarily. This may look to be extremism with the appraisers. Is it really? But I have a question to eyebrow-raisers: Is making of good work-culture not involve all from top to bottom? If yes, then those who are at the helm of affairs should also be appraised for their accountability towards the making of that work-culture. Second, when the students can appraise their teachers, what is wrong in teachers appraising their seniors/appraisers? As the students can provide an effective feedback on the effectiveness of their teaching skills, general behaviour, quality of teaching etc. similarly the teachers too can give feedback to their appraisers/ seniors provided they can welcome this revolutionary change. When we say that appraisal is two-pronged process, we mean appraisal of juniors by the seniors and vice versa. Appraisal system applies equally on all: From top to bottom and bottom to top. And who can be the best appraiser of one another other than those who are actively involved in the process. It will not be an exaggeration if we call managers and teachers/workers two wheels on which moves the cart of appraisal system. If one wheel goes missing, the cart cannot move any further.

1.8   Preparation for Successful Performance Appraisal:

There are several tools to be used for the successful completion of appraisal process. Therefore, they should be kept ready before setting on the appraisal process. Among these tools are: Self-appraisal pro forma, Self-checklist, Pro forma for pre-appraisal discussions (interviews), Appraisal key, Appraisal pro forma, Key for External Appraiser etc. Appraisal of teachers should not be entrusted with external appraisers. It is best left to the Principals, Vice-Principals, Headmaster, Senior Teachers and other educational experts from the department. Teaching being an art can be properly and successfully appraised only by educationists. Second, they are very much familiar with the social, economic, cultural and other background of the institution; they will be able to do a realistic appraisal which will be more useful to provide the feedback. It will be more useful if the appraisal by the department is made on the following grounds:

> ➢ Appraiser and appraisees should sit together and plan the appraisal scheme with mutual consent.
> ➢ All should be well aware of the appraisal goals and their significance.
> ➢ Appraiser ought to assure the appraisee about maintaining the confidentiality of the appraisal results. It should remain between the two only.
> ➢ Appraiser should ensure the appraisee about maintaining objectivity in the appraisal scheme.
> ➢ Making an environment conducive to an objective and unobstructed appraisal is the responsibility of the appraiser. He should ensure it throughout.

➢ Informality, honesty, positivity, creativity and smooth communication between the appraiser and the appraisee are other prerequisites of a successful and all-round appraisal.

The above description shows the significant role the appraiser plays in any organisation. Therefore, he should be competent and capable enough to adept himself to the prerequisites of appraisal and understands its psychological and sociological nuances very well and gives them proper care. That's why the appraisers should be very well trained so that they become experts. Preparation of appraisal-pro forma, interviewing and appraising etc. is no less than an art. So the appraiser needs to be perfect in this art. Keeping these things in mind, all the organisations need to make proper arrangements for the training of the appraisers so that they could be successful in implementing the appraisal procedures. Appraisal tools have to be faultless. If the tools are not good, how can they give the desired results?

1.9   Who Should Appraise the Teachers?

Now the question arises who should appraise the teachers. Readers/ listeners may laugh at the question as this responsibility lies on the principals, headmasters and other senior officers. But no: This is not true. Appraisal by only the seniors may suit industry but never in education. Reasons are obvious. Teachers' performance skills pull the strings of the whole society: Young and old, girls and boys and; parents and children. Therefore all have a right to appraise the effectiveness of the teachers' skills of teaching. They have not only a right but also have competence to do so as they are in direct touch of the teachers and know them threadbare. Besides principals, senior officers and educationists, there are students, parents and other elders of their families who come in close contact of the teachers. And the first appraiser is the teacher himself. He should self-appraise.

➢   **Self-appraisal:**

This is the most difficult appraisal. It is an old saying: It is easy to find fault with others but very difficult to find one about self. And self-appraisal means finding one's own faults. Only those who can make use of this wonderful exercise, are adept in "self-observation" and "self-actualization" and are keen to take up this exercise. This art of self-appraisal is rare. Teachers are always engaged in deep thought but they too lack introspection which is the first step towards self-appraisal. Second step is self-discipline. When the teachers are self-disciplined, only then they can use their all skills and energy to self-appraise. Self-appraisal is not self-glorification or self praise but studying one's own behaviour in a particular area: In case of a teacher it is important for him to know how much effective he is as a teacher. If he finds any fault with his teaching methodology, he is supposed to remove it himself voluntarily. Here it is important to point out that this exercise of self-appraisal becomes very easy for those teachers who honour their students' views about their teaching because it is quite natural that the students know better than anyone else about the effectiveness of their teachers' teaching skills because they are the ones who are directly influenced by it. To highlight the importance of the feedback by the students, I quite often used the concept-related humour saying as the wife knows her husband by each pore; similarly the students also know everything about their teachers. So the teachers must honour the opinion of their students. At this, on one side the pupil-teachers used to laugh hilariously, on the other they imbibed the importance of their students' opinion in a natural way. Their faith in the students' opinion increased.

➤ **Teachers' Performance Appraisal by the students**

Teachers continue to evaluate regularly their students as a part of their duty but they never want to assign this job of appraising their teaching skills to students because it seems to them very risky. Most of the teachers fear that giving such a liberty of appraising them to the students will not only make them outspoken and undisciplined but they will also lose their control over their students. Their teaching skills will become hot topics for tongue wagging in households and streets. They also say that students and parents do not know what education means, being inexperienced they do not know what to appraise and also do not know how to appraise; and therefore giving such responsibilities to them will be inappropriate. May be their fears are true to some extent but our opinion is a bit different. My experience says that such fears are expressed as an excuse only by those teachers who are not competent, reach their classes unprepared, do not have any academic topic to discuss with the students and therefore waste their teaching time in gossips. Such teachers should never forget that students are psychologically very intelligent and they can easily see through the weaknesses of their teachers and even parents and they (such teachers and parents) have to bear young ones neglect. On the other hand, the teachers who work honestly, go to their classes fully prepared, do not waste a single minute of the students in class, make the best use of each minute in teaching and perform their duties sincerely, get full respects from their students. It will not be an exaggeration if we say that such teachers become an apple of their students' eyes. Such teachers leave an indelible impression of ideal role-models on their students. They never disobey them. The students never forget such teachers and consider them as their sincere well wishers.

Actually the students know a lot about the teaching skills of their teachers. It is another matter whether they express it openly before their teachers or not. If the teachers invite their views, they will provide invaluable feedback from which the teachers can gain and learn a lot. If the teachers do not make use of this easily available source of feedback on their teaching skills, then they are depriving themselves of the invaluable information. The appraisal by the students is not confined only to their teaching skills but it also includes the teachers' relations with their students, their parents, fellow teachers and so on. The teachers can benefit from such information very much. Therefore all the educational institutions looking ahead of the times must make such informal provisions from which they could know what the students and parents think about them in general and the teachers in particular.

> **Teachers' Performance Appraisal by the parents**

In our opinion, after the students if there is any other one to appraise the teachers, it is the parents. They are the 2nd most significant source of feedback about the teachers' teaching skills, their general and classroom behaviour with their students and their general image in the educational institution. Teachers must avail this reliable source voluntarily because the parents will never lie as they have entrusted their wards to the teachers provided the teachers give the parents liberty to express themselves without any fears. To benefit or not to, depends only on the teachers. They will have to express their intentions for it before the parents if the teachers wish the parents to open up.

It is true that all the parents may not be competent to appraise the teachers and their teaching skills or may not have time to spare for this intellectual job, still there may be at least 30-35 % parents who will certainly be competent to do this rational and thoughtful work on the basis of their wards' feedback about their teachers' work and conduct. It is common among parents and the students to discuss school college affairs freely in their homes from which the parents gather such information which may be very useful for the teachers for their professional development. The students never feel the freedom and fearlessness with anyone else which they feel with their parents while discussing their teachers work and conduct. Therefore the teachers must establish a rapport at least with such enlightened parents who can help them "to know themselves at least professionally" and know what their students feel about them and their work. It is often seen that the parents make their opinion about their children's teachers on the basis of what is told to them and there will be no harm if the teachers take the first step to know about it. It will rather improve their image among the parents. It will be pertinent to emphasise here that all that is retold by the parents may not be true. In that case, the point of difference may be discussed with the informing parent so that he in turn may educate his child. This type of deliberation may go a long way in maintaining a cordial and collaborative atmosphere in the institution. After all, students and parents satisfaction is the most important objective of the educational institutions.

> **Peer Appraisal**

When an experienced and skilled senior colleague appraises his fellow-teacher, it is called peer appraisal. It may be performed by a single teacher or by a group. Forward looking management makes the maximum use of this type. This kind of appraisal has its advantages as well as disadvantages. Since the peers are very well aware of their colleague's plus and minus point, his way of working, his attitudes and know the ground realities of their departments, such an appraisal may be objective to a large extent. As regards disadvantages, the peers may give undue favour to their colleague as they have to work with each other and for each other.

> ### Teachers' Performance Appraisal by the Management

Last but not the least important performance appraisal is by the management. It is the most popular and most used appraisal-technique. In this the appraisal is done by an officer to whom the teacher is accountable. He may be his Principal, Headmaster or any other departmental Education Officer. The appraiser makes a thorough appraisal and prepares his report. Whoever does this appraisal, he ought to be honest, candid, creative, sympathetic, sensitive and expert in the art of appraisal. This appraisal can be reliable and dependable only if there is an unflinching faith of the appraisee in the appraiser. As soon as this faith gets demolished due to any reason, the appraisal will become worthless. The appraisal by the management has one advantage in as much as it helps in manpower management of the institution as it provides encouragement to the teachers through appreciation of good work, assists in the audit of existing staff and further planning. But it must be noted that the teacher always desires to be appraised on the basis of facts. If the management keeps it in mind while doing the appraisal then the teaching skills of the teacher concerned are sure to improve as it will double fold their confidence in the management and interest in the organisation and they will make the best and maximum use of the results of their objective appraisal. This appraisal could be by:

- Any senior.
- Two seniors.
- Any senior on the basis of previous appraisals.
- Any outsider authorized by the management.

Whoever may be the appraiser, he needs to keep all the conditions discussed herein above for an ideal appraisal in mind while performing this important job otherwise the exercise will be useless.

CHAPTER 2

Performance Appraisal in Education: Special Discussion

Performance appraisal referred in management literature is not of much relevance in the education sector. Its reasons are obvious. In trade and industry, the product is perceptible. It can be easily measured. Its quality can be tested scientifically and can be presented as reliable evidence. But it is not so in education. There is lot of difference between the products of trade/industry and education. The reasons for this are: —

2.1 Difference between Industrial Performance Appraisal and Educational one

➢ In trade/industry, conditions at workstation can be easily controlled but it is not possible in education. In education, circumstances change very swiftly and the teachers cannot exercise effective control over them.

➢ In trade and industry, raw material is used; quality of which could be easily maintained which will ensure good production. But in education it is not so. Here the raw material is children whose receptivity changes every minute and the teachers can do very little in this regard. Here the teacher (the producer) and the taught (the product): Both are human beings and belonging to two different generations with different values. Human-nature is very complex which cannot be controlled as machines and the raw material in industry.

➢ In trade and industry, the production is machine based but in education, it is not so. Here the raw material is the student and the producer is teacher both of whom being human beings cannot be controlled as in industry.

➢ In trade and industry, the raw material can be procured from its best sources and regions famous for them but it is not so in education. The students have to be taken from a limited area.

Their family, social, economical and cultural background differ drastically upon which depends their receptivity, a prerequisite to good learning. These differences cannot be reduced overnight leaving the teacher helpless.

➢ The teacher is also a human being and he cannot be controlled machinelike. Teachers' family, social, economical and cultural background, his personal problems, work conditions etc, too have a great influence on his work. If all these are good, his work will be good. If not, his work will suffer or be of average standard.

Due to the reasons mentioned above, the products by the teachers are students' accumulated knowledge, their general conduct and behaviour, tendencies, creativity, character and overall personality which cannot be easily measured like the products in trade and industry. For example, the number of bulbs and their quality can easily be measured but how can we measure the changes in the students' attitudes the same way. In education, production based salary system cannot be applied like that in industry.

In fact, teachers work should be appraised with reference to the circumstances prevailing in education and not on the basis of the product or procedure. It makes it abundantly clear that the standards and procedures of appraisal in trade and industry cannot be applied in education. Its appraisal is possible and relevant only in educational environment and with academic reference.

In trade and industry where lifeless raw material is shaped into a new product is quite opposite to education sector where sensitive and moody (whether due to personal nature or social, domestic and academic influences) students' behaviour, habits, ideas and thoughts are refined through constant counselling so as to make them useful members of the society. Not only this, neither teaching has an equal effect on all the students nor does the teacher influence them equally because of their social, economical or cultural backgrounds. Besides, the receptive faculties of the students also differ from each other, sometimes very drastically. It has also been observed and academically admitted that the students are more influenced by some negative and extraneous social non-educational factors like films, television, internet etc than by their parents and teachers. If the student comes under the sway of negative factors, it becomes almost impossible for the parents or the teachers to free him from it and engage him in studies seriously. All his efforts in this direction go waste. And for this we or the appraiser cannot blame the teacher. As an example, take the family environment of the student. If it is disturbed, the students coming from such families will certainly be obstinate, spoilt, hostile and careless. On the contrary, the students from peaceful families will be docile, receptive and sincere to whatever they are asked to do and the teachers' work will become very easy.

Therefore, the educationist will have to develop such appraisal methods which can take all such factors mentioned above in account while planning teachers' performance appraisal. The techniques being used in trade and industry cannot make a successful appraisal of teachers who have to deal with sensitive and young living beings. It is also important that the teachers are well informed in advance about what has to be appraised and with what methods.

Successful performance appraisal can be possible only if appraisers and the appraisees are very well aware of the institutional goals. These goals ought to be challenging but not unmanageable and unachievable. Goals should be assigned according to the qualifications, experience and talents of the teacher. When the goals and objectives are made clear before the teachers and they have understood them well; then the techniques and procedures of their performance appraisal should also be placed before them and thoroughly explained. Thorough knowledge of these techniques, methods and procedures will make them perform effectively. Following are the principles of educational performance appraisal:

2.2   Principles of Educational Performance Appraisal:

> ➤ The appraisal should be related to the teachers' work. It is often seen that the teachers are engaged in non-academic works as well like census or as election booth management which have nothing to do with education. Such odd and irrelevant jobs should neither be appraised nor tagged with the areas of

appraisal. In our view the teachers should never be burdened with such works as these may affect their teaching skills badly.

➢ The objectives to be appraised should be challenging but not unachievable. It is true that the challenging objectives ignite the zeal of the teachers but it does not mean that the appraiser has got the rights to overburden the appraisees with unmanageable and unachievable objectives. These will discourage them. Therefore the objectives to be performed should not be too difficult and arduous. Once it so happened that a newly appointed teacher, who had no experience in addressing the morning assembly, was abruptly called on the very first day by the Principal to address the students. The teacher performed satisfactorily and spoke on "Punctuality." But the big question arises whether Principal was right and justified about what he expected from the inexperienced teacher? I fail to understand the motives of the Principal: Whether he wanted to test the teachers' knowledge or he wanted to demoralize him? Whatever his motives, I am sure that it at least was untimely.

➢ The area to be appraised should be told to the appraisee very clearly so that he could concentrate on his desired goals, use all his faculties in achieving the same and could visualise the difficulties coming his way well in advance and find solutions to them. Arjun in Mahabharat could hit the bird's eye only because he was clearly told where he had to hit and he was absolutely clear what he had to do. So the appraiser and the appraisee should be clear about what they have to do lest there is any doubt.

➢ The goals ought to be objective and specific. If there is any uncertainty about the goals, it will certainly create doubts and the teaching works will suffer. The goals should be objective. There should be no subjectivity while setting the goals because only objective goals can be related to the work-specific. It will be easy for the teacher to achieve the objective goals.

➢ The area and quantity to be appraised should be time bound. The time available to the teacher for the completion of work should be quite clear so that he could complete the work within assigned time.

➢ It will be excellent if the goals and the appraisal principles are written down. Unwritten goals and principles may create doubts and differences at a later stage because it may give rise to subjectivity and loss of objectivity which is a prerequisite to ideal appraisal. Subjectivity if creeps in, will put a big question mark at the appraisal and defeat the purpose.

➢ Educational goals and appraisal principles should be contextual and need-based. If they are out of context and irrelevant, they cannot appraise the educational goals and objectives. For example, if the appraisal principles used in trade and industry are used in education sector, they will be ineffective and meaningless. Ingvarson and Chadbourne (1974) say that teacher-performance-appraisal has two main purposes.

- The teacher should be responsible and accountable. They should be able to say what they are doing and what their goals are. It will be ideal if the teaching is student-centered because the ultimate goal of education/teacher is the all round development of the students. If the teaching is not student-centered, the teacher is accountable to explain the logic of such teaching. He should tell whether his teaching is not going in the wrong direction? And if they are aware of it, why are they doing so? They need to explain all this necessarily.

- Second, the teacher ought to be progressive, engage in self-study, update their knowledge continuously and continue to refine their teaching methodology. This performance-appraisal is a never-ending process. One of the aims of teachers' performance appraisal is their professional development. Therefore the appraiser ought to provide ample time and opportunities to teachers for professional self-development. The teachers, who desire to do research, ought to be provided all necessary facilities: Time, financial support and opportunities. The teachers should never feel that hurdles are being created in their professional development. "These two purposes are not mutually exclusive. Each is a facet of professional responsibility."

Both of these two purposes are evaluative and development centered which look to be similar but in reality are not. Scriven calls them "Summative Evaluation and Formative Evaluation" respectively.

2.3 Cycle/Procedure of Performance Appraisal

This cycle or procedure is prepared after carefully studying the appraisal system, its peculiarities, identifying prospective problems, methods to be used for their solutions, finalizing the tools to be used in it and the way quick feedback to be given soon after the appraisal. This cycle can pass through the following stages:

A. Pre-appraisal Stage:

This is the first stage which consists of several activities. The possible ones are:

- Explicit identification of the departmental goals and their clear delineation.
- Specific listing the departmental activities.
- Responsibilities of each member of the department to be clearly assigned.
- Establishment of the principles of the appraisal system.
- Preparation of performance appraisal pro forma and clear statement on its application. Should be preferably given to the appraisees in writing.
- Orientation programmes to be prepared for the appraisees.
- Distribution of performance appraisal pro forma to the appraisees.
- Schedule for discussion (pre-appraisal interviews) to be fixed.
- Even after the orientation programme, liberty to put any question about the appraisal process should be given to the appraisees.
- Doubts if any on the above to be removed.

Appraisal could be successful only if the complete transparency is maintained with regard to its principles and measurement scales, clearly defined and explained to the appraisees. There should be no doubts about anything otherwise its results will be incredible and ineffective and will never yield the desirable fruits. When the principles and measuring scales of appraisal are clear like in trade and industry, the results too are trustworthy, clearly visible and very effective. But in the educational sector, it is difficult to establish them, especially the measuring scales, so precisely. The reasons of this have already been discussed earlier. Even then, some principles and a few measuring scales can be determined so that the appraisal of the institutions and their different departments could be successfully done. For example, the appraiser can easily discuss the appraisal procedures, appraisal areas; appraisal objectives etc. with the appraisees and establish workable standards of mutual understanding so that the educational goals and objectives could successfully be achieved.

The appraisal pro forma should be prepared with much care because the success of appraisal system depends almost on them.

B.   The Appraisal Stage:

It prepares the stage for the preparation of the pre-appraisal discussions (interviews) and appraisal portfolios. It ensures:

> Whether the goals which were settled after assignment of duty and work, are being achieved on not.
> Whether the appraisal methods cover the analysis of professional acumen of the teacher.
> Whether the appraisal methods are able to identify the strong and weak areas of the teacher's performance.

This stage is very important part of the appraisal process as it includes the pre-appraisal discussions (interviews) with the appraisees. It promotes "participative management" which removes all the fears or reservations of the appraisees about the appraisal system and its motives. The appraiser becomes a fellow traveller who knows the ways and the directions they have to go and guides other fellow travellers i.e. the teachers how to improve their performance and the teacher, feeling encouraged by the brotherly guidance, puts all his efforts in his professional development. It is widely accepted when the results of an objective appraisal are put before the teacher, he gladly accepts them. He does not hesitate in accepting his weaknesses because the appraiser shuns criticizing him. On the contrary, he helps him identify his weak areas and suggests how he can strengthen them on the basis of his own experience. Instead of saying your work is bad or good; he puts the results before the teacher and asks him what he has to say about them and what more can be done to improve them? This approach establishes a rapport between the teacher and the appraiser very fast and probability of starting a mutual discussion over the weakness will increase. At this moment the appraiser may come forward and ask the teacher what he could do for him. Such friendly approach may pave way for the self-correction by the teacher considerably. If the appraiser succeeds in creating such cordial atmosphere while appraisal process is on, it will be his biggest achievement for him as well as the institution and the appraisee will also feel proud.

It looks normal and natural also. When one exhibits interest in one's own weaknesses, it looks as if he is trying to self-appraise himself or sharing his own appraisal process with the appraiser. Need of hour is only that the appraiser puts the results of appraisal before the appraisee in a very friendly, cordial and objective manner. He should not force his opinion on the appraisee. Let the results of the objective appraisal speak themselves, show the teacher his true picture like a mirror and make the teacher realise about the need for improvement. In such a situation, the appraisee also feels the need of improvement in his performance and sincerely tries for the same.

The performance appraisal pro forma should be prepared jointly by the appraiser and the appraisee. Necessary confidentiality must be observed. But the appraisee should not feel that he is being kept in dark intentionally or with mala fide intention. In such a scenario there is every possibility of suspicion raising its hood between the appraiser and the appraisee which will be a deterrent to an ideal appraisal killing the purpose of the exercise. Therefore, the appraiser must ensure that the preparation of the pro forma for appraisal should not smell of officialism.

C.　Post-appraisal Stage:

This stage studies the post-appraisal scenario with reference to the following:

> To find out whether the performance appraisal system helps the appraisee to exercise control over his incompetence and further improves his competence.
> To share those theories and methods with all which assisted in achieving the targeted goals.
> To make necessary amendments in the theories, principles and methods in the light of post-appraisal experiences.
> To prepare a plan for appraisee's professional development with reference to the feedback received during post-appraisal discussions (interviews) with the appraisee.
> To ensure that the performance appraisal continues as it is a non-stop exercise.
> Whenever a need is felt, informal discussion are made so as to keep the tempo going.

2.4　Self-appraisal:

When the teacher observes his teaching himself, evaluates it effectiveness, judges his competence and makes efforts on his own to remove his incompetence and further enhances his competence if found to be standard, it is called self-appraisal. It will be excellent if this exercise is carried out monthly. There is no other good exercise than self-appraisal provided the teachers are trained by the department in this art. The author's own professional views are that there can be no other system better than self-appraisal in the educational sector. Appraisal made by others in education sector is often looked at with suspicion because they are considered untrustworthy.

2.5　Logic behind Self-appraisal:

> Teaching is a performing art which is more a mental and intellectual activity than that performed by educational tools. It is a combination of several skills. Only one skill will never

suffice. The teacher has to choose which skill to be used, when and with what objective? It is the teacher alone who knows why he used any skill; not anybody else. Each teacher's teaching methodology will be different. Each teacher's personality is distinguished and whatever he does, including teaching will certainly be affected by it. But any appraiser will appraise the teacher in a given frame keeping all these factors out of his appraisal strategy. Therefore, self-appraisal is the best option in the teaching profession.

➢ Teaching is a creative activity. And there is no denying the fact that creativity differs from one person to the other. Secondly, creativity can be well appraised and appreciated only by the creator, none else. If anyone attempts at it, it will not be accurate. For its valid appraisal, the appraiser needs to be equally creative if not more than that. Secondly, it is the creator only who is competent to decide after the self-appraisal why, how and where to improve the appraised task.

➢ Since the teaching is a creative activity, it requires a deep sense of art, an imaginative mind, sensitive vision, firm grip over expressive power i.e. through words and body language. Similarly, the appraiser should also be equipped with these qualities if he wishes to be a successful teachers' appraiser. He should be an appreciator of art (teaching being an art: Like an art of expression on stage), highly conscious, imaginative, sensitive and thoughtful. If the appraiser lacks these qualities, how he can successfully appraise a sensitive activity like teaching.

➢ The art of teaching cannot be casted in a mould. It is a purposeful human-behaviour. It is an artful trial of one on oneself for others who are in the learning stage. It makes him a good or poor performer. Agree that there are teachers' training colleges which train and prepare future teachers. But except imparting some technical knowledge to the trainees, what more they do? As we have said in the foregoing paragraphs, the teacher needs to be sensitive, imaginative, thoughtful and a language-skilled expert. Do these teachers' training colleges do anything in this direction? And these days the teachers' training colleges are in such a poor mess that even the lecturers have no command either on their mother tongue or the foreign language or any other language. What and how they teach or train is anybody's guess. Actually these qualities develop from within when one wishes so or with increasing experience. Appraisal of such a delicate job by someone else seems to be expecting too much from the one who may not possess these essential qualities.

> The teacher is also required to be a stage-performer because he may have to use his facial expressions, eyes and limbs movements; and the pitch of his speech to make the points clear. He has to master the art of Role-playing. In the views of the author, the teachers' training colleges do nothing in this direction. These are learnt and developed by the teacher passing through various stages of his teaching career over a time. Appraisal of such skills could also be done by only those who know their importance, is competent to appreciate and appraise them; and to give logical suggestions in their improvement. Self appraisal is the best in teaching sector.

> Teaching directly affects the learner but its effect on each learner is not the same. The fact is that the effect of teaching cannot be same on each student because each one is unique as a person/learner. Some are fast learners whereas any of his colleagues may be slow or average. Some are too slow. How a stranger-appraiser who does not know anything about these variations can appraise the teaching of a teacher? Under these circumstances, only the concerned teacher himself can appraise his methods of teaching and the effectiveness of the skills he used to teach the entire group and or uses to bring the slow learner at par with others.

But we do not mean that there is entirely no need of supervisors or appraisers for teachers' appraisal. Need still exists otherwise who will train the teachers in self-appraisal or ensure whether the self-appraisal has been conducted sincerely and honestly or not and whether the weak areas detected during the self-appraisal were addressed for self-reforms or development or not.

We only mean that it would be most appropriate due to the reasons mentioned above if the teachers are trained in self-appraisal. It will not only ease the task of the appraiser but also boost the morale of the teachers. Their self-confidence will increase gradually and feel more responsible to the duties and accountable to all the stakeholders i.e. the students, parents and the management.

2.6   Procedure of Self-appraisal

A.   Pre-appraisal Stage:

This is the first stage. Teachers' Self-appraisal procedure may be almost the same which is applicable to appraisal by others and given above. The only thing that we want to repeat is that the self-appraiser has to be very sincere, honest and conscientious person; and never forgetting that he has a great responsibility to perform. Steps are:

- ➤ Getting thorough knowledge of institutional and departmental goals.
- ➤ Setting personal goals on the basis of these goals.
- ➤ Indexing of the institutional activities.
- ➤ Clear understanding of the responsibilities.
- ➤ Clear understanding of the principles of self-appraisal.
- ➤ Preparation of pro forma for self-appraisal.
- ➤ Providing its copy to the senior or appraiser-observer.
- ➤ If needed, arranging an orientation programme for the self.
- ➤ During the orientation programme, the self-appraiser should practise the following :

  - • Select a sub-topic.
  - • Collection of additional material/information.
  - • As far as possible, the knowledge should be given through concept related humour.
  - • Should stand before a looking glass and practise topic related body movements to prepare for the real role-play.
  - • Prepare himself how he will encourage the students to actively participate in the teaching.
  - • Other preparations like providing feedback, class-work selection etc.
  - • Discussion with the supervisor.
  - • Making everything clear with regard to the above.

B.   The Appraisal Stage:

This stage is used to prepare the records for discussion (interview) with the supervisor and of the appraisal. Here the self-appraiser has to ensure:

> ➢ Whether the educational goals related to his assigned job are being achieved or not.
> ➢ The self-appraiser has to analyse his work from a professional point of view during the discussion with the supervisor.
> ➢ What precautions the appraiser should take to make the self-appraisal a brilliant success. He may spell out to the supervisor what precautions he has already decided to take whereupon the supervisor may further suggest if need be.

The self-appraiser will have to be very honest with reference to his performance and present his mistakes or weaknesses before the supervisor candidly. He should never forget that he is self-appraising himself and what its importance is for him as well as the institution. He will have not only to identify his minus points but present and admit them honestly before his supervisor. He should also be ready to spell out the ways and means to overcome those weaknesses. If he faces any difficulty in identifying his weak areas or is unable to find ways to improve his performance, he should never hesitate to consult his supervisor so that the problems could be addressed to.

C.   Post-appraisal Stage:

This stage deals with the situations after the self-appraisal with reference to the following:

> ➢ To find out whether the self-appraisal process could be effective enough to identify the weak areas of the self-appraiser.
> ➢ To share those principles and techniques which helped the self-appraiser in making his self-appraisal a success?
> ➢ To make amendments and refinements in the principles and techniques of self-appraisal on the basis of one's own experience if need be.

> On the basis of the feedback, such schemes to be discussed with the supervisor for their formulation which ensures the professional development of the self-appraiser.
> On the basis of the feedback, the supervisor and self-appraiser should take such steps which may ensure continuity of self-appraisal and professional development of the self-appraiser.
> The supervisor and self-appraiser should continue their informal discussions (interviews) for the institutional developments.

As said earlier too, self-appraisal should be monthly so that the teacher could self-appraise himself on the basis of small units of the teaching-material regularly. Appraisal by the supervisor may be half yearly. Such appraisal will provide effective feedback on the results of the self-appraisals which will not only help the self-appraiser but give the institution an opportunity to see if the technique of self-appraisal is doing any good to the teachers and the institution or not. In our opinion, if this cycle of monthly self-appraisals and half-yearly appraisal by the supervisor continues regularly, it will boost up the morale of the teachers, lessen the burden of the supervisors and improve the academic environment of the institution. The logic behind this hypothesis is clear. On one hand it gives morale-boosting liberty to the teacher, on the other it gives desired opportunity to the supervisor to judge the effectiveness of the scheme, lessens his burden and spares a lot of time to think and plan for further institutional growth and development.

2.7   Role-Play: A Note

Effective teaching-learning could be possible only through active participation of the teacher and the taught. Therefore, teaching through interactive role-playing will be more effective than lecture method. The author's professional experience also supports this theory. He had come across such an appraiser who himself had role-played during his model-teaching and influenced the author to such an extent that he immediately adopted the role-playing technique for teaching. He had taught the story "The Giant and the Garden" in English in such a humorous way playing the role of the giant that the students laughed a lot, enjoyed the teaching very well and impressed the author too much. Surprisingly, the responses of the students to the probing questions put later were excellent proving further that role-playing teaching laced with germane humour pay rich dividends. The appraisers should also pay due attention to this aspect of teaching. Role-play is that technique of teaching which presents a real or imaginary human problem in a dramatic manner through verbal expressions and body language. It can be effectively used in education as well. It includes concept-related facial expressions of eyes, lips, tongue; limb movements of head, hands, feet or any other body parts; concept-related expressions of *Ras* (sentimental expressions) like anger, love, hatred etc. In our opinion, if a teacher wishes to be an ideal teacher, he must learn the art of role-playing. He should be a good actor.

2.8   Qualities of Role-play:

There is no doubt that role-play in teaching will be welcome by the students due to its fascinating dramatic qualities. As we all know that the speaker who uses body language and concept related humour while delivering his speech, is liked most, similarly the teacher who uses these techniques while teaching, will also be most popular among his students.

2.9   Features of Role-playing:

(i) **Activity oriented:** Any thought or concept has to be put in action. For example, if 'A' has committed any mistake and has to beg his pardon from 'B' then 'A' will go to 'B' and actually ask for it. How effectively he does it and motivates others to learn the art of begging pardon depends on his efficiency as a teacher.

(ii) **Supports human relations:** Role-playing sensitizes others about the skills of maintaining them in the same way as a player does about the skills of his game.

(iii) **Tendency modifier:** When a person is placed in noticeable situations, his tendencies tend to change fast and have to act as behaviour is not only related to his personality but to situations as well in which one is put by circumstances. For example, when the Head of school asks any teacher all of a sudden to address the students in the assembly.

(iv) **Promotes awareness to others sentiments:** How others' sentiments are affected by any particular role, is well conveyed through feedback. How scolding a student publically embarrasses him is well highlighted by it.

(v) **Trend setter:** Critical analysis of the effects of sentiments expressed openly encourage for better and socially acceptable behaviour. For example, a female teacher's expressed ire against any misbehavior will motivate the erring student to modify his conduct.

(vi) **Removes negativity:** Helps identifying and rectifying the shortcomings. Suppose anyone is habitual of passing remarks on others. If he is put at the receiving end, he is most likely to change his habit after tasting the cutting remarks.

(vii) **Introduces Professional control:** Role playing teaches how sentiments are to be socially controlled. When an appraiser is put in the place of an appraisee, he can easily feel the negative tendencies of an appraiser towards appraisees in a professionally acceptable manner.

❑❑❑❑

CHAPTER 3
Performance Appraisal: Guidelines

Educational institutions utilize the services of self-motivated experts and dedicated scholars in their field so as to make the best use of available human resources for conducting educational research, facilitating institutional development and achieving other goals easily. All the staff members of the institution will have to keep these goals in mind all the time and continue to work for their achievement.

3.1   Philosophy of Performance appraisal:

The management will have to introduce half-yearly or yearly performance appraisal system in their institutions so as to provide feedback on the performance of each teacher with reference to his performance and their institutional goals. On one hand, it will remind the teachers of the institutional goals and on the other, they will modify their working for improvement with reference to the feedback. By their improved performance, they will essentially do better for the achievement of the institutional goals. The main objective of performance appraisal is to maintain a balance between the teachers' personal and professional expectations and the institutional goals. The performance appraisal could be at the department level also. The departmental performance appraisal is considered as most important activity for institutional development because it further improves the performance of the teachers because the focus of the whole exercise centers on the department. It makes the teachers more productive and creative thereby improving the work-culture of the department in particular and the institution in general. Therefore the performance appraisal is to be a continuous and non-ceasing activity. The techniques and procedures of performance appraisal may differ from one department to the other but their goals and objectives will be the same which are as follows: —

> To ensure each teacher's contribution to the departmental development.
> To speed up the professional development in the department and the institution.
> To promote policies ensuring teachers' professional development in the institution.
> To acknowledge the contribution of teachers in the institutional development.
> To reward the teachers for their role in the institutional development.

3.2   Desired Objectives of Performance Appraisal Philosophy:

Manpower management consists of a lot of activities. But hopefully, they need to be designed and developed on the basis of needs of each department so that the targeted goals could be easily and successfully achieved. Not only the departmental needs should shape these activities, but these should also be modified according to the times, circumstances, technological changes and immediate causes otherwise the performance appraisal systems will fail.

Performance Appraisal systems will be successful only if:

> They are transparent.
> Teachers' and appraisers' responsibilities are very well defined to minimize doubts.
> Expectations from both are clearly explained.
> Performance Appraisal systems are regularly updated and are kept open for further improvements.
> Free and uninterrupted interaction between the teachers and the appraisers.
> Teachers are clear about the significance of the performance appraisal for their professional development.
> Appraisers are also clear about the importance of the performance appraisal for the institutional growth.
> The Performance Appraisal is absolutely objective.
> Its records are kept properly and used for individual, professional and institutional development.

> Teachers' related issues may be guided by their performance appraisal but ought not to be directly affected by them.
> Professional development and opportunities for it must be linked to Performance Appraisal.

3.3   Accountability of the Organisation:

Each organisation should permit performance appraisal of its employee at least once a year. If it is implemented, each department or its unit will be responsible for an appropriate and suitable performance appraisal of each of its member. For this, each department or its unit will also be tuned to relevant and needful changes in the performance appraisal systems from time to time. The human resource department must ensure the above.

Senior officers' and performance appraisers' appraisal will have another important component and; that is how much useful is the performance appraisal of their subordinates conducted by them to the growth and development of the institution/organisation. Other components of the seniors' performance appraisal will be:

> Effectiveness of their performance appraisal policies and principles for institutional and individual goals.
> Quality, relevance and adequacy of outcome of the teachers' performance appraisal.
> Usefulness of the teachers' performance appraisal for the organisation/institution.
> Reliability of their performance appraisal.

The human resource department ought to provide the following facilities for seniors' performance appraisal:

> Arrange for the training of the appraisers, provide relevant literature and recording systems/gadgets like video recorders.
> Opportunity for the regular study of the performance appraisal to gauze its effectiveness for the institutions and for further improvement in the procedure if need be.
> Preparation of the performance appraisal pro forma and their safe upkeep for use and other purposes like highlighting the

profile of the institution and the organisation. It will not only showcase the institutional image but will also assist it if any legal eventuality arises.

➤ Preparation of each teachers' or employees' dossier which must contain all relevant records including performance appraisal reports and the teachers' or employees' efforts to improve his work with reference to the feedback after each performance appraisal.

3.4 Formal Performance Appraisal:

The analyses of the annual performance appraisal fully depend on how effectively and efficiently have the teachers and appraisers prepared for it. Formal performance appraisal procedures must include the study of previous performance appraisal report, their feedback and follow-up-actions; and the scheme of institutional goals for future.

3.5 Procedure of Annual Performance Appraisal Review:

In order to achieve the desired results of the performance appraisal, following points have to be kept in mind.

➤ **Review of previous achievements:**

It will have to be ensured whether goals set earlier were achieved or not, and if not achieved, what were the reasons like difficulties and obstacles in the conduct of the performance appraisal. This is the time when failures in achieving the desired goals are collectively analysed and all possible efforts or guidance for improvement is made to remove the road-blocks or the bottlenecks, successful employees are identified and unsuccessful ones are singled out to guide them on their shortcoming and encouraged to remove them for better performance. Goals are again redefined very well so that everyone understands them. It brightens up the future of the institution/ organisation. Further the performance appraisals, their analyses and feedbacks will be more successful, fruitful and effective. This is the time when teachers/employees are encouraged to use new techniques or motivated to work on new projects and schemes. Moreover, it is necessary to assess the workload of each teacher/employee objectively before asking for working on new projects or schemes. Priorities must be fixed on the basis of their significance for the institution and the unimportant ones should be dropped.

> ### Discussion on Professional Development:

Under it, what the employees/teachers expect from their appraisers or the organisation for their professional development is discussed mutually. It establishes their faith in their superiors which is very important for both. This is the moment when the appraiser tries to understand the teachers'/employees' expectations and place them before the management for consideration so as to maintain cordial relations between the management and the grass root workers/teachers and also for making efforts for their professional development.

> ### Documentation:

The appraiser, making particular reference to these components of performance appraisal, should prepare appraisal records and keep them safe. Fully and very well understanding the performance appraisal scenario along with the expectations and achievements of the teachers/employees, the appraiser must make their special mention in the performance appraisal report. The teachers/employees should not be in dark about their performance appraisal. They should be very well aware of their abilities, efficiencies and proficiencies including deficiencies so that they could try remove them with reference to the feedback. Copy of this performance appraisal report must be made available to the teachers/employees. It will create an atmosphere of mutual faith, speed up the improvement process and improve the performance appraisers' image in the eyes of the teachers/employees.

> ### Safety of Records:

Each department of the organisation should develop a scheme to keep these records safe. Every performance appraiser should also learn to maintain these records so that they are at their hands while analyzing them. Such records need to be preserved at least for five years. These ought to be maintained at departmental and Headquarters' levels. At the Headquarter level, it should be kept by human resource department. These documents are normally very confidential and only the concerned top officials who are responsible for smooth functioning of the organisation should have approach to them. These documents should be accurate and complete in all respects as they may be produced before the legal authorities or statutory bodies in case of their demand. All personnel related matters like increments, promotions, demotions, suspensions etc. being contemplated should strictly be made on the basis of these records to avoid any contradictions between the documents and the action taken. The truth is that the improvement in the expertise could be possible only by thorough knowledge of appraisal and the under mentioned appraisal skills:

- Setting institutional goals.
- Setting goals which could be measured.
- Interactive skills.
- Appraisal and record-keeping skills.
- Counselling and providing feedback skills.
- Listening skills.
- Team raising skill.

3.6   Performance Improvement:

In today's educational scenario, the sense of accountability lacks. It ought to be as it is the key to success. When the students' performance is evaluated with a sense of accountability, their performance will certainly move upwards and the teachers too will start performing on their teaching assignments in a better way. Both will be more alert to their work: Students towards studying and the teachers towards teaching. By the teachers' better teaching and testing skills there will be remarkable improvement in the students learning skills which in turn will better the overall image of the institution, raise its standards gradually and the possibility of achieving the set goals will considerable increase.

3.7   Logic behind Performance Appraisal:

Performance appraisal is considered to be that practice which keeps an eye on the performance of the teachers' teaching skills and keep their records properly and regularly so that personnel related decisions could be taken quickly and objectively. It also facilitates quick decision making process through mutual discussions on education related issues. Thus Performance appraisal establishes a rapport between the teachers and the management through its performance appraisers. Teachers too feel responsible for policy-making. Collective responsibility increases though it may differ according to time, place, situation or kind of job. This removes all the doubts about each other's roles in the institutional system, for the development of appraisal systems, techniques, procedures and tools and preparation of appraisal reports, and its overall upkeep. In case of need, a role-document can also be prepared which is often termed as "Code of conduct."

The aims and objectives of the performance appraisal could be well understood by the gains that an organisation enjoys after its successful accomplishment. Mohrman, Lawler and Resnick-West emphasise the following advantages: —

> Boosts up the teacher/employee for better performance. It is thus a powerful motivator.
> Fills the teaching community with self-esteem by inviting them for participation in the whole performance appraisal process.
> Encourages self-introspection among the teachers and appraisers about their work-attitudes.
> Develops new insights among teachers and supervisors/ appraisers.
> Establishes effective communication among appraisers and appraisees.
> Increases creative thinking among the teaching faculty and educational administrators by creating conducive atmosphere for the same.
> Clarify the goals of all stake-holders very well.
> Boosts up collective understanding among all stake-holders about the organisational, professional and individual goals.

> ➤ Develops a healthy practice of rewarding for good performance.
> ➤ And most important. It increases faith in the whole team: Starting from top managers to the grass root workers.

3.8   Policy Statement:

Each member of the organisation should participate in the performance appraisal processes and procedures. It would also be pertinent if a separate scheme/plan is prepared for each teacher or employee. As the personnel development plans are designed collectively, similarly appraisers and the appraisees ought to work together for the development of performance appraisal system.

While reviewing the performance appraisal results with reference to the teachers' duties and responsibilities, organisational or institutional and departmental objectives should be kept in mind. Not only this, expected benefits could be derived from the performance appraisal processes only if these are supported by timely revised policies, aims and objectives.

Since performance appraisal is very important for any organisation/ institution, each teacher ought to be appraised at least once a year. It will also be pertinent for the appraisers to remain in constant touch with the appraisees throughout the year. It will help them to know the teacher individually and thoroughly; and should continue to interact with them, and counsel them whenever and wherever need arises and monitor their work. All this exercise should be strictly in tune with the aims and objective of the organisation.

3.9   Appraisal: Modus Operandy:

During the performance appraisal processes the following points should be kept in mind: —

> ➤ Pre-appraisal meetings should be held to discuss the performance appraisal procedures.
> ➤ Teachers should utilize this opportunity to apprise the appraiser with their aims and objectives.

> In the light of these objectives, the appraiser should fix the time limit for the performance appraisal.
> Keeping these aims in view, pre-appraisal of classes to be taught should be carried out which will help the teachers to revise their objectives.
> Post appraisal meetings should be held and the methods and procedures of the performance appraisal should be reviewed in the light of experiences.
> A comprehensive report of performance appraisal which ought to include performance standard of the teacher and its time limit be prepared.
> A copy of the performance appraisal ought to be given to the teacher.
> In seriatim documentation of the records ought to be kept.
> Concluding meeting of the teacher with the appraiser wherein he could openly discuss the report with the appraiser.

3.10   Rapport and Appraisal:

Appraisal experts have termed the aloofness of teachers from the whole process or their disinterest in the appraisal schemes as their narrow-mindedness which hampers professional and individual growth. But it also exhibits the orthodox approach of the management which fails to invite the teachers in such an important exercise. This tendency deprives both of them of the latest trends in education and they have to depend on their limited resources to solve their professional problems. But the teachers are less responsible for such isolation because the managers or the policy makers never like to include them in the process. The policy makers are more confined to their ivory towers while making educational policies thus ignoring the teachers who are more familiar with the ground realities. The policy makers make policies without knowing studying the factual position and thrust them on the teachers. Its immediate fall out has to be borne by the teachers and the long term one by the students. The present educational scenario in the country fully justifies it. Educational policies are such which give bookish knowledge to the students but fail to transform the students into good human-beings. It is just because the policy-makers consider them "super-think-tanks" and feel it below their dignity to consult the teachers who are the real makers of the Nation.

Hargreaves (1991) says that teacher collegiality and collaboration are not merely important for the improvement of morale and teacher satisfaction but also for "teaching to be of the highest order" and to ensure that the teachers make use of each others' experiences "to grow during their careers". Teachers' collegiality thus improves professional as well as institutional growth. Though the teachers are never consulted by the curriculum designers, still they religiously implement the curriculum without which (the teachers' support) it could never have been executed. It is highly positive on the part of the teachers that they implement the educational policies thrust upon them from outside. Since they have to implement these policies which are framed at central level they work together to achieve their objectives. If this type of sense of collaboration among teachers had been missing, all educational policies would have dashed to the ground.

Thus the teachers play a leading role in every respect at the school/ institution level. Today the educational institutions are motivated to use modern methods of management using decentralizing techniques for taking important decisions thus instead of monopolizing, the leadership is shared.

Teachers' collegiality is two dimensional. First, sharing each others' experiences and collectively benefiting from them. Second is the collective responsibility of the senior most and the teachers in implementing the educational policies.

Traces of teacher collegiality are often noticed in day to day school/college activities. Among them are staff-room discussions, collaborative planning, team teaching, peer teaching, mentoring each other, research and collaborative action research. These activities are a mix of various programmes aimed at achieving the objectives through mutual interaction and collective efforts and they go a long way in developing a work culture.

The exponents of collaborative teaching say that it develops a culture of sharing at the institution level wherein teaching values, habits, ideals, confidence further develop along with the updated techniques of teaching which improve teaching. But this type of collaboration gets disturbed where unity of thought lacks among the school faculty and these differences escalate to such an extent where establishing contact with each other becomes highly volatile.

Collaboration also gets blurred with political interference. Teacher collegiality which rests on understanding each other and moving forward to help each other is highly disturbed when political elements pollute the ideas which sometimes result in high-jacking of values appropriate for educational institutions, thus harming the total atmosphere in the institution and resulting in movements, strikes and chalk-down-agitations. It badly vitiates the whole teaching atmosphere.

The managements which are broad-minded deal with such problems with an open heart and mutual understanding thus not only maintaining the collaborative environment but also promoting it to a desirable extent thus making the political influence almost ineffective. The authoritarian ones also succeed in controlling the situation by using dictatorial methods but this peace is of the "peace of graves" which may disrupted at any moment on a tiny issue. The first one develops a culture of sharing whereas the latter thrusts it upon the teachers from outside. System forced from outside violates individual rights, disturbs peace of mind, suffocates, causes irritation, kills initiative and creativity.

Just opposite to it is the collaborative culture which facilitates development of democratic values preserving individual rights and promoting imaginative faculties, improving creativity and above all a work-culture that unites the entire teaching faculty to achieve the set goals. One thing to be carefully noted in this context is that in India, we have a true democracy. Then why do the most of the educational institutions here are highly volatile and are not in a healthy shape? Simple reason of this is the absolute political control over students unions, teachers unions and sometimes even on the managements which continue to vitiate the academic atmosphere achieve their nefarious goals. The less said about the selfish motives of these political outfits, the better. They can do anything, anytime and anywhere to gain their political mileage. In such a surcharged atmosphere, and a "Disruptive-work-culture" how "Collaborative-work-culture" could be replaced easily. Therefore the managements of educational institutions, the teachers and all other workers must ensure that their institutions which are meant for the character formation and personality development of the new generations do not fall into the hands of crafty politicians and become a war-theatre. The democratic values which I have mentioned earlier are inter-school and intra-school values which help not only the teachers but also the students to assimilate them to be responsible citizens. It is the needed positive way to teach the students lessons of democracy. It revitalizes the collaborative culture and educational atmosphere gets recharged for creative activities. Hargreaves (1991) analyses both types of cultures and has arrived at the following conclusion: —

3.11 The Culture of Voluntary Co-operation: Characteristics:

• **Spontaneity:**

This culture is the direct outcome of spontaneous self-realisation of the teachers for cooperation. Motivation for it is from within. It may be from outside too but it will be democratic thus honouring the will of the teachers and boosting their spontaneity which drives them to work with mutual cooperation.

• **Voluntary:**

It is out of one's own will in nature. It is not forced through orders or dictates from outside but emerges from conscientiousness and willingness because it is found to be more productive, useful and job-satisfying.

• **Development Oriented:**

In this work-culture the teachers work together as they are self-motivated to achieve the goals fixed by them. They set their priorities keeping their professional and institutional goals in mind which keep motivating them to work together. They might be getting moral support from outside that is from their seniors but the main motivation is from within: That is we have to achieve; and they ultimately achieve which they had set out to.

- **Free of time and space**

Collaborative work culture is free from the limits of time, space and place. There is a self-generated system to regulate the work but the teachers are free to make suitable and appropriate modifications in it. The self-generated system is only to assist them but not to overrule the teachers. In this system, when, where and what the teachers do does not matter much until we have their results. All work goes on in an informal manner. The teachers work according to their conscience. Actually this system works on the assumption that the teachers being self-conscientious keep working on their own in the larger interests of the learners and the institution.

- **Unpredictability:**

In collaborative cultures, the teachers keep a tab on their work themselves therefore they are free to take a decision. In such a situation, the results can never be accurately predicted. Another reason for this unpredictability is its being student centered. Teachers move according to the pace and needs of the students. It is the main grouse of the educational administrators of centrally implemented schemes that the teachers have too much liberty in this culture and the policy-makers feel neglected. That is why at the school level where most of the educational policies are centrally made and implemented, the schools are deprived of collaborative cultures labeling it impracticable, irrelevant and unsuitable because of the centre's control over all affairs. In other words the teachers have no say or participation in policy making or curriculum designing whereas the centrally made schemes could never be implemented without the cooperation of the teachers who are continuously ignored. It is perhaps the only reason that in centrally-controlled cultures, there are protests and agitations quite often. Neither the authorities wish to lose control nor do the teachers acclimatize with such stringent regime.

Table 1
Collaborative versus Forced Cultures

Characteristics	Characteristics
Spontaneity	Centrally controlled
Voluntary	Compulsion
Development Oriented	Implementation-oriented
Free of time and space	Fixed by Time and Space
Unpredictability	Predictable
Free to Experiment	Status quoits
Democratic	Authoritarian

3.12   Characteristics of Forced Culture:

The features that characterize the forced culture are the following: –

- **Centrally controlled:**

In forced cultures the implementation of policies is centrally controlled and the educational institutions or the teachers have no say at all in it. These being centrally controlled, whatever development takes place in them, it is not spontaneous or natural but fully guided and monitored by those who know nothing about the ground realities or the difficulties the students or teachers face in day to day functioning or the implementation of the schemes. Priorities may be the same which the collaborative cultures have but their nature of implementation makes all the difference. Teachers' or students' have to abide by the dictates; and the teachers seem to be happily working but with a grouse at their hearts. They show their willingness unwillingly.

- **Compulsion:**

Forced cultures are management driven and the teachers have to abide by their orders. The teachers are not free to take any decisions. They cannot modify any educational scheme if the need arises. They are tied to the schemes forced upon them from above. The teachers fear pay-cuts, demotions or other penalties if they try to go against the schemes even in case of need. Therefore, there is no option before them except toeing the line of the superiors. Thus forced culture is fully "forced" upon the teachers from higher authorities through the Principals.

• **Implementation-oriented:**

In forced cultures the whole institutional set up is tied to the programmes chalked out by outsiders that are the policy makers and the teachers look to be working in tandem. The explicit orders are of the Principal but on the behest of implicit ones of the school board or State department of education. These are national educational policies which may be relating to national school curriculum framework or interactive learning; but are implemented through the Principals and teachers who have no options of their own. And in this context it is evident that centrally sponsored educational programmes too cannot be implemented without the collective cooperation of the teachers. It is the environment that makes the difference: Here in forced cultures the environment is often found to be suffocative because it provides no freedom to teachers to change their teaching strategies even if the need arises.

• **Fixed by Time and Space:**

Forced culture is time and space bound. It is administratively controlled. The teachers have to finish the assigned work in the given time which, in case of teaching is sometimes not possible. For example, if the class is slow and low performer, how can the teacher stick to the time limit. He will have to slow down his pace which he can pace up only at the cost of the students. It poses another question: Whether the students are for the educational system or the system is for the students. Obviously the honest answer will be in favour of the latter. Not only this, the educational seminars and workshops look to be collectively organised but they too are bound with time and place which the teachers have to undergo.

- **Predictable:**

The forced cultures can predict precisely what they expect from any activity. It is another matter that such predictions too may go haywire and questions may be raised on them due to lack of collaborative environment. On explicit plain, it seems that forced culture ensures educational and professional development but inside story is different. Since the teachers cannot be innovative, the cognitive, imaginative and creative faculties get jammed. How then the professional growth could be possible. Its bad effects are visible on the students too. All continue to work like machines. Another fall out of this trend is that most schools have been turning into business houses. Teachers' cooperative attitudes depend on the quality of the nature of their performance appraisal and their professional and institutional objectives. But the forced culture kills this too because the senior teachers along with the head of the school are often found making a group and the juniors are forced into another left-out group. It spoils the entire atmosphere thus killing the initiative. The juniors start considering themselves useless and feeling insulted. How can effective performance appraisal be carried out and professional and institutional development take place in such a charged atmosphere. These are not at all possible with teachers' cooperation and freewill. Unjustified, biased and guided by non-educational purposes performance appraisal can never initiate mutual understanding.

- **Status quoits:**

Since forced cultures do not give freedom to experiment, these are by and large status quoits that is they maintain the established order. Innovations are shunned and the beaten track is preferred.

- **Authoritarian:**

Unlike collaborative cultures which adopt liberal ways, the forced ones are thrust upon the workers from higher-ups. It is therefore more authoritative and daring to go against it is considered a taboo.

❏❏❏❏

CHAPTER 4

Managerial Vision of Teachers' Performance Appraisal

All organisations have their aims and objectives for which they are established and they try their best to satisfy their clients accordingly. Be it hospital or an industry, be it telephone or postal department, or be it a college or any training institution, all are on their toes to ensure that their customers are fully satisfied. For this they equip their organisations with the latest technology and other equipments, on the other hand they hire the best available manpower most suitable for their organisation, make arrangements for their on-job-training using the latest industrial or educational trends; educating and preparing them for the latest trends in performance appraisal. Performance appraisal is that technique by which the organisations try to make, maintain or boost up their image among the stake-holders and ensure all that their organisation is capable of providing the world class services in the relevant field and the best service conditions to their personnel for their individual and professional growth so that they could feel fully attached with their organisation and render their best services for the organizational growth and development. Such steps are necessary because the organisations image is not made by the best of available infrastructure but by its fully satisfied efficient and proficient dedicated workers.

Most of the organisations carry out evaluation of work on annual basis. These analyses are confidentially conducted by senior officers and are most often kept under wraps and the assessed are not at all informed. In fact the latter have no participation in such evaluating exercises. These analyses are labeled by different people with different nomenclatures. Most common among them are: Annual Inspection, Performance Analyses, Performance Appraisal, Staff Developmental Analyses and Personnel Analyses. The word "analyses" is quite often replaced by "review" also. Whatever these terms may be called, all except "Performance Appraisal" refer to work-evaluation of the workers which is quite often one sided and without any participation of the concerned worker. Contrary to these one-sided exercises is the "Performance Appraisal" which the managements widely accept these days due to its broad approaches to making performance policies, chalking out its implementation procedures, setting short and long terms professional and institutional goals etc. involving the appraisees in the process. Another difference between others and the "Performance Appraisal" is while others emphasise on performance the latter on development.

4.1 Performance Review:

"Performance Review" aims at short-term goals which could be achieved in a short time with surety. This review is quite often based on the achievement of organisational goals, quality of the product and the employee's capabilities. Feedback is provided later so that the reviewed gets to know about his shortcomings and try to overcome them for better performance which ultimately benefits the organisation with better production.

4.2 Staff Development Review:

"Staff Development Review" focuses on present and future working-skills and capacities of the workers thereby making arrangements for their need-based on-job-training. Personnel's professional development is its central point. The employees are provided all possible opportunities and facilities for it. Such programmes are frequently held which facilitate staff development. These include educational workshops, seminars, symposiums, discussions, debates and research. Teachers or the employees are sponsored for higher education in national and international institutes. Special study leave not only with full benefits but with special grants for higher education or educational research are granted. It, on the one hand enhances the skills of the teachers, on the other brings good name and fame to the institutions concerned.

Briefly speaking the former is work-centered whereas the latter is employee-centered. But in our view this type of differentiation is more academic than real. They cannot be separated like this.

Both are interrelated. Work needs worker and the worker the work. One cannot exist without the other. Yes, it will be excellent for the institution as well as the employees if their personal and profession development is kept in view while framing institutional/ organisational policies which will benefit both in the long run. If the working capabilities and capacities of the employees are increased, their performance is sure to be better, thus boosting the image of the organisation/institution.

The term "Appraisal" is more acceptable these days because it includes not only review of work but also employees' development; and also because a single word expresses the concept precisely in the shortest way. Readers may be aware that the use of this term has been opposed off and on. "Staff Development and Appraisal" is suggested quite often in its place. Still the term "Appraisal" has been widely accepted due the reasons mentioned above.

4.3   Individual and Organisational Needs:

In order to assimilate the work force in the organisation, performance appraisal is one the most effective technique. Every worker enters any organisation with his pre-determined goals and dreams of fulfillment of his personal needs. These goals and personal needs work as guiding forces to perform at his work well because this tendency gives him satisfaction. Among these workers, most are those who are too ambitious and wish to achieve the maximum like promotions and money in the minimum time. But there are few who not only perform well at their job but also perform for extra time to finish the task assigned to them because these achievements give them extra satisfaction and more happiness than that which the former get through promotions and money.

Most often the workers have to face the challenges of records set by their senior or former employees. The organisations too face this challenge but with a different angle. They have to make arrangement for manpower fully competent not only to achieve goals but also to keep the record of those already achieved goals intact and strive for further betterment. The employees' goals and the organisational goals confront with each other. Through the process of objective and collaborative performance appraisal, an effort is made to integrate both. Such process of "integrating the individual worker with the organisation" satisfies both. The employees feel emulated whereas the organisations feel great in emulating their employees because it eases the organisational pressures on workers for better performance. Benefits of this process ultimately reach the organisations.

There are several ways for the **Effective Integration** of the employees with the organisation. These are: —

> Selections, appointments and induction.
> Training, re-training, delegation and mentoring.
> Promotions, salary, bonus and rewards.
> Counselling, guiding, quick grievance redressal mechanism and disciplinary actions.
> Performance appraisals and feedbacks.
> Lay off pre-discussions.

Establishing unbiased match between the individual and organisational goals is very difficult if not impossible because both are poles apart. Consequently the opinions differ. Sometimes these divergent views may be overt and at other covert. These are dangerous in their hidden form and may harm the work-culture of the organisations. In these circumstances, it is the obvious duty of the organisation to take such steps which may detect the dissatisfaction and disagreements, find a acceptable remedy to them, increase the faith of the employees in their organisations, establish rapport between both and an environment conducive to growth and development is established. Such steps will be good for both especially the organisations. The strategies for establishing such cordiality may differ from department to department.

Now every organisation knows very well that good performance does not entirely depend on employees' abilities and capabilities but also on the facilities available to the teachers, the mutual cooperation in the employee-peer-group and the management. It is now widely acknowledged and accepted that supportive co-workers and the seniors when working as a team on a common goal bring excellent results. They can bear with the tensions or anxieties more comfortably and establish a rapport more easily than those who work alone or have no cooperation among themselves. The group members boost each others' morale because this approach serves a common cause. It serves not only the common cause but the institutional cause is also well served by such collaborative cultures as it improves the entire working environment at the work-place. It improves cordiality among all irrespective of the status. Though there appraisers and appraisees but the appraisal system being based on mutual understanding creates such an atmosphere that everything seem to be informal.

Corporate psychologists and sociologists have reviewed the individual goals and needs in a meaningful and pragmatic manner which if followed, can bring unexpected and fruitful results in the form of increased quality production. There is no doubt that the age of the employee, his personal and social status, his financial needs and family background make changes in his personal needs and direct his personal professional goals. For example, the needs and goals, work and responsibilities, achievements, sentimental attachment with organisation of middle level manager will be in the centre of his work approach. Contrary to it, a lower lever worker's needs and goals will be entirely different which by and large will be more financial and related to his family and its daily needs.

Besides the above important considerations, it is the most important for the institutional success that the teachers are very well informed about their roles and responsibilities and other related issues like: —

- ➤ What are institutional expectations from the teachers?
- ➤ How these expectations could be fulfilled?
- ➤ How much freedom to take independent decisions is available to them?
- ➤ What are their roles in setting institutional goals?
- ➤ What are their responsibilities, prerogatives and limitations of discretion?
- ➤ Nature of performance appraisal schemes.
- ➤ Feedback system.
- ➤ How feedback could be useful for the teachers in particular and the institution in general.

> What are morale boosting schemes like rewards for good performance.

Such orientation of the teachers would not only be necessary for better performance but also improve the performance appraisal systems and integrate them to the organisation.

4.4   Organisational Management Styles:

McGregor (1960) has hypothesized bi-polar views of the organisations to look at their employees. They are X-Theory and Y-Theory.

> X-Theory: Such organisations are bureaucratic and hierarchical in nature and they look at their employees as work shirkers, ambitionless hence require coercion to be active at work. They are more interested in security of their jobs than performing on them. Therefore, in order to please their superiors they use other ulterior techniques like flattery. Being unsure of the employees' commitment to their work, the managers keep a close eye on them to see what they are doing. They do not let the employees get together. They make such rules and keep the employees in such situations that they do not come into contact with each other. Such authoritarian managers do not allow any employee to stay in one place or department for a long time lest they start forming groups or develop closeness. In such suspicious environment, the employees become completely dormant, insensitive and work like machines. They take no interest in work on their own because their ideas, thought-process and imagination get curbed. Creativity is the first casualty in such an environment. Status quo is maintained by all. No one wants to take any risk by taking any initiatives.

> Y-Theory: This is just opposite to the X-Theory. The managers after explaining the institutional or organisational goals to the employees and getting to know the individual goals of the employees develop such a culture at the work place that every employee starts taking interest in performing the duties to the best of their competence. According to Dennison and Shentor (1987) the employees listen to their conscience and work according to its dictates rather than of their seniors. The

employees in such an environment are self-disciplined and they need no coercion to work. They feel an emotional attachment with their organisation. They are more imaginative, creative, take initiatives for betterment of their organisation and are therefore more research-oriented. They are more encouraged by feedbacks and rewards on their good performance. Consequently, such an environment not only facilitates individual and professional growth of the employees but also ensures organisational and institutional development. Quantity and quality of the product improves and the organisation gets name and fame in the society.

Good and development oriented organisations adopt a middle path between these two. Since both are poles apart, the former curbing creativity and initiative and the latter giving too much freedom to the employees, are at their extremes. So to maintain good image and improve it further, it is preferred progressive managements to be moderate on both counts. Burns and Stalker (1968) suggest a model consisting of good characteristics of mechanical and cooperative theories. The mechanical theory is defined as " . . . suitable to hierarchical management structure in which there is a clear definition of assigned roles, formal and mainly vertical communication and a built-in system of checks and supervision."

The Organic theory on the other hand is "designed to adapt to a rapid rate of change, to situations in which new and unfamiliar problems continually arise which cannot be broken down and distributed among the existing specialist roles. Relationships are therefore lateral rather than vertical, and form and reform according to the demands of the particular problem."

Though there is a growing interest of the management of the educational institutions in developing collaborative work cultures or establishing organic style of management but the pace of this change is very slow as the dictatorial forces still keep dictating their terms due to their rigid attitudes and their lack of faith in the work-force. It results in creating hurdles in the all round development of the institutions. Such contradicting situations are created which are opposite to each other. Policies are forced from above. The teachers who are the real implementers of all educational policies are ignored at each step. Neither at the policy framing nor at curriculum making stage are they invited to participate. They are kept in dark till implementation stage. If the teachers are involved in policy framing or curriculum designing, they will naturally feel more committed to their implementation. A glaring example is the emergency era of the nationalist leader Mrs. Gandhi's times. Family-planning, though a very useful national scheme which had affected the teachers as well as the students to a great extent, crashed to the ground only because the teachers who were assigned to get it implemented, were never consulted while framing such an important policy of national importance. A positive step resulted in negativity because the teachers, the torch-bearers of social change, were not consulted at all. Unfortunately such participative and collaborative management is not considered so far to be a part of performance appraisal which in reality is.

4.5 Organisational Scenario and Appraisal:

Organisational scenario can be defined as an amalgamation of various work cultures the employees possess in an organisation irrespective of the kind of structure, be it hierarchical, bureaucratic, informal, dynamic, risk-taking or static. Undoubtedly the structure of the organisation do affect the work-culture of the employees, still they maintain their identity freeing it from the structural influences. This culture gets nourishment from the individual values and experiences of the employees which they import from outside after joining a new organisation. Seniors having such values too affect their work-force and gradually enrich it with their own norms and experiences thus playing pivotal roles in its cultural development. The employees and seniors are thus mutual contributors in this healthy process. They leave an indelible good impression on the organisation scenario. Contrary to it, employees' negative values may do the same but in a negative manner.

A strong will of the management to integrate the employees in the organisation too plays an important role in determining the integration process, its methodology and its efficacy in the integration of the new employees in it. Most of the organisations do it as quickly as possible but their ways of doing it differ according to their cultural climate. The hierarchical managements do it fixing the employees within their set rules whereas the dynamic ones adopt the principles of giving desirable freedom to the employees. The former feel that they make the employees whereas the latter believe that the breathing space given to the employees lead to innovations speeding up the process of qualitative professional and institutional development. The former thinks that any delay in the integration process will spoil the work force, the latter feels that integration ought to be as natural as possible so that the creativity of the workers is not curbed. The latter welcomes new ideas and suggestions. Dynamic organisations are so liberal in their approach that they do not hesitate even to make use of the informal feedback on their performance from their juniors and learn a lot from it. Hierarchical managements do just its opposite. They never welcome new ideas. Suggestions or feedback from the juniors are a big "No." Consequently, there are deadlocks. There is no communication between the managements and the work-force which always reels under desperation and depression in such situations. They start feeling useless in the organisation. They do not take any interest in the work. The little the better: Becomes their motto at work. And the organisation becomes "sick."

To get rid of such situations created by a hostile scenario, the technique of performance appraisal facilitates integration of the employees with the organisation and whets its wits inspiring it to meet the employees' personal, economical, social and psychological needs. By such pro-employees' approach the organisations set on such path which leads to achieving organisational goals fully: And if not fully; at least partially because they get the active support of fully contented and high-spirited employees. If the organisations neglect the employees and their interests, quality and quantity of the production is bound to fall. Performance appraisal centering on only the employees' interests too will be favourable for the organisations as the contentment levels of the employees will motivate them to put in their maximum efforts for the good health of the organisation. And the performance appraisals centering on the interests of both are sure to render the best of output. Therefore, for the welfare of both, the individual and organisational goals ought to be integrated well and made explicitly clear at the earliest.

4.6   Appraisal Process: Its Limitations:

Appraisal cannot be limited into narrow boundaries. Its scope is vast. On one side it identifies organisational goals, its needs and expectations, on the other it aims at knowing the individual needs, priorities and expectations of the employees; and thereafter facilitates integration and collaboration between both. Sometimes, the performance appraisal may focus on both simultaneously. Undoubtedly, it too is concerned with the employees' professional, social and economic development but it also ensures their acumen in doing some special assignment or work. These works and assignments are decided either by pre-appraisal discussions or work-specification thereafter.

It is well-known that the individual development and performance appraisal are interlinked. If these are not, then there is no use of any such exercise as they would just become eyewash. Performance appraisal does not mean only mean making a decisive opinion about any employee or his performing skills but also eliminating the possibilities of taking subjective judgments or on the grounds of hearsays and gossips which quite often haunt most of the organisations and which are mostly baseless. How anyone can become supportive in professional development of a teacher until he knows the weak areas of the beneficiary very well. Similarly how can an institution move forward on the progress-path until its plus and minus points are not very well appraised. It will be like prescribing medicines without diagnosing the ailment. Successful teaching-appraisal could be possible only when educational achievements of any institution, complete profiles of its successful and unsuccessful teachers, its inter-faculty collaboration, its students-teachers relations and rapport between them and its ability to change according to the students or the situations are well-known.

Performance appraisal ought not to be linked only with assessing the capabilities and abilities of the employees. It is more than this. If the managements keep other aspects like promoting talent by giving timely rewards and promotions of it in mind, it will be very useful to their organisations. Tomlinson (1992) has rightly emphasized its other significances which enumerated below.

4.7   The Appraisal Potentialities:

It is observed that well designed and better implemented performance appraisal schemes give better results.

- Well defined goals create a sense of belongingness among the employees.
- The employees feel self-motivated for professional development.
- It increases a sense of self-confidence and self-respect among the employees.
- Free discussions facilitate mixing up. It lessens aloofness among the team. Conflicting views are limited. Leading to consensus.
- Develops collaborative work culture.
- Facilitates professional consultations.
- Speeds up collective efforts to achieve organisational goals.
- Brings individual goals in sync with the organisational goals.
- Provides opportunities for resolving issues feedback discussions.
- Helps in examining and analyzing institutional roles.
- Helps the educational managers in giving positive directions to the teachers according to the educational goals.
- By conveying the institutional goals to the employees very clearly, it speeds up collective efforts in achieving them.
- It re-energizes the employees.
- It creates open and transparent atmosphere and helps consultations from top to bottom.
- It provides such an atmosphere that even a single employee can leave a good impression on the organisation if he is capable to.
- Thus it brings the talent in the open.
- Establishes morale-boosting and rewarding atmosphere.
- Facilitates integration among the employees and organisation.

The above mentioned benefits cannot be gained from one technique. Institutional and organisational environment directly affects the work culture and the employees' behaviour at work. An organisation that has firm faith in its employees gets their fullest cooperation and reaps rich dividends from this positive approach. Another one which emphasizes in the employees' self-development and gives them freedom to engage in institutional work soon finds positive energy flowing through the organisation. Yet another one having minimum resources at their disposal uses them in such a way that they achieve their goals in spite of constraints. Gist of the matter is that success lies neither in the rich resources at hand nor in the huge work force at the workplace but in sound strategies that the managements apply to back up their employees and motivate them for further improvement in the achievements and in the healthy environment in which the employees work. Besides the performance appraisals too mean different in each organisation. One looks at it as a technique for self development. Such institutions make such steps part of their performance appraisal which ensure the professional and individual development of the employees. Such organisations put the employees on such jobs and in such a manner which provides them opportunities for their development. Another one may go for maximum output from their employees without giving an iota of thought to their professional and individual development which may quite often alienate them from their organisation.

It is almost unthinkable to have a single approach which may ensure all round development of all the stake-holders: teachers, students, parents, institutions and organisations. Even if we invent such a scheme, we will have to make suitable changes in it according to time, space and other circumstances. If the performance appraisal is time and efficiency bound, its area will be limited and will be unsuitable on a larger scale. Therefore it is necessary for performance appraisal that its goals should not be contradictory. They should be in sync to each other. The more contradictory goals we have the more resources will we have to arrange and make use of. Performance-appraisers ought to understand this point very well that their objectives should not be in conflict with each other. They ought to focus on institutional as well as professional-individual developmental objectives simultaneously.

4.8   Kinds of Staff-Appraisal:

Pre-appraisal discussions (interviews) are of four types. They are Development Centered, Management Centered, Laissez fair and Judgmental. But none can be termed as excellent. It will be wishful thinking that anyone type meets all the characteristics. Yes, it is possible and feasible also that we use one type for some advantages and another for other types. It is also important to decide how much weight is to be given to professional, individual or institutional development. In other words, it is the management which has to decide whether professional and individual development has to be focused more; or the institutional development should be prioritized. It will have to decide whether the employees are more important or the organisation/institution. It will also have to fix the roles of the management and the employees. In other words, how much freedom should the employees have to be given in taking decisions, in setting their goals, in deciding performance appraisal objectives, in identifying training needs, in deciding developmental strategies, in taking responsibility or they are to be guided by managements' dictates? Characteristics of all the four types are given in the following table No. 2.

Table 2:
Kinds of Pre-appraisal Discussions

Development Centered	Management Centered
• Is professional, collective and collegial. • Aims at holding moral, ethical and professional values. • Adopts peer appraisal techniques. • Adopts mutual approach for self-improvement. • Takes collective responsibility for making schemes and achievement of objectives. • Aims at long-term professional development. • Self-development oriented. • Self-motivating. • Integrates with the organisation very fast.	• Is authoritarian and hierarchical. • Aims at doing and achieving by dictates. • Appraisal through managerial team. • Uses rewards and punishment theory indiscriminately. • Sets targets for maximum organisational output. • Concerned with short-term goals. • Diminishes employees' self-confidence. • Management dominated. • Causes alienation with the organisation.

Laissez Fair	Judgmental
• Permits self-development. • Gives relief to the managements from responsibility. • Allows employees to raise issues. • Requires less direction from the management. • Self-motivation oriented. • Gives ample opportunities to the employees for self-correction. • Improves creativity among the workers. • Increases accountability. • Progressive.	• Uses appraisal to control. • Decision making rests with the management. • Data based evaluation of employees. • Often compares low achievers with high achievers. • Extrinsic motivation essential. • Merit rated and performance-related salary fixing. • Lacks creativity. • Lacks accountability. • Regressive.

Managerial appraisals are quite often rightly criticized. Managements' too much interference with the day to day functioning of the organisation often kills the employees' initiatives. Policies, objectives and targets are frequently changed thus jeopardizing the smooth process of functioning or appraisal systems. Employees who are the real implementers and achievers are sidelined and are left demoralised. They have no say in policy-making and no liberty for taking self-decision in case of obstacles coming their way while performing. Every time they have to look towards their seniors for guidance or direction. Consequently the employees also start shirking responsibility. All these factors weaken the managerial appraisal system. In education sector these days, it is emphasized that performance norms should be standardized. Even then there are areas in which targets or objectives could never be possible identified or set. That is why such areas cannot be properly appraised as well.

It is encouraging that the management norms are now being humanized on the basis of workers' psychology. Consequently, employees' importance for an organisation, their autonomy and significance for self-actualization is being recognised. Further, it has made the employees/teachers aware for their professional development and organisational/institutional objectives/goals. So they set their individual objectives keeping the institutional objectives in their mind reducing any chances of conflict. This new scenario which is slowly gaining ground ensures development of both: The teachers/employees and the institutions/organisations. The teachers make use of all their talents and abilities to achieve their goals: Institutional and individual. They do not shirk responsibilities. Rather they come forward to bear responsibilities or to share them. These are good signs for all the stake-holders.

Keeping these progressive and revolutionary changes in performance appraisal systems in the education sector in view, we will have to accept that very few teachers are capable of self-appraisal without any support from the seniors or management mentors. In educational institutions, these mentors could be friends senior in age and experience or any other senior who may appraise the strengths and weaknesses, abilities, capabilities and special skills of a fellow teacher and provide objective feedback to him for self-improvement: May be in consultation with the appraiser. Such appraisals could be truer than those done by very seniors who may harbour unrealistic expectations from the teachers. Colleagues just senior to the appraisees could be more informal with them and appraise not only the teacher well but also the working conditions and ground realities which directly affect teaching work. In some institutions, the appraisal is done by senior managers or the appraisers hired from outside for this purpose. But being very senior or a stranger to the appraisee and unknown to the ground realities, they will not be as effective as the peer-group can be.

Keeping these essentialities of performance appraisal in mind, the education sector has become more sensitive to the teachers' professional growth and development and has started voluntary appraisals in place of the forced ones. The teachers, finding these new adaptations suitable for their professional growth, also have welcomed these changes. The teachers have also started realising that updating of their teaching and self-appraisal skills will transform their caliber as well as the educational institutions into centers of learning and add to their professional and institutional glory which will be advantageous to all the stakeholders especially the teachers themselves and their institutions.

4.9 Perspectives of Appraisal in Teaching:

There are three perspectives of teachers' performance appraisal. The appraisal systems also exhibit those beliefs and experiences which are related to the professional practice and development. Both these perspectives are significant which cannot be ignored. First is of Schon (1983, 1987, 1991) which is called "Technical Perspective", "Reflective Perspective" of Elliott (1985, 1988, 1991, 1993) and Reflective Practitioner Perspective (Bridges et al.1986)

➤ **Technical perspective:**

In the technical perspective, practice is more prominent. The more one practises with reference to predetermined standards, the more efficient and expert one becomes. The problems coming in way during such practices are overcome with the help of pre-determined standards, past experiences and set objectives. Thus the "practice" is well organised and exercise is made on the basis of already-tested skills and experience. In teaching profession, experienced and skillful people impart knowledge after testing it on the basis of formal curriculum through traditional, protected or diluted training which they earn during their teaching. These curricula are designed on psychological principles and the teaching practitioners practise it in an informal manner. These practices are analytical, sensible and usable which are governed by the principles of providing motivation, feedback and reward/punishment. It believes that performance can be improved as desired by using carrots and sticks.

➤ **Reflective Perspective:**

According to the reflective perspective, the exercises that are undertaken are first judged, properly measured and if needed, it is modified according to the requirements. Most important aspect of this perspective is that the problems that crop up during practice are considered to be solvable by the teachers themselves on the basis of pre-earned knowledge, experiences and skills. Such problems are grouped in a category of solvable ones. The problems which still persist and cannot be solved by the teachers are researched and diagnosed upon. New experiments are made. And through such innovative approaches, their solutions are found and standardized after which this new knowledge is imparted/shared with the teachers. This new knowledge then becomes a part of earlier knowledge bank.

Teaching practice is carried under general laws so as to reach determined and defined goals. This process is well regulated; pre-determined and fully transparent which can easily be measured and standardized so that effects of the exercise could be appraised. This process separates the objectives and the available resources. Hence it is close to the technique which could be practically utilized. What is needed most is the acceptable scale on which qualities of teaching could be measured. If it is done, these standards could be used for imparting training. The appraiser too can use them objectively and impartially when appraising the teaching performance of any faculty. Aware Teacher-trainees use teaching skills and the students' reactions (informal feedback) to their work as stimulants. In order to find solutions to problems coming in their way of teaching are handled on the basis of the teachers' earlier experiences and knowledge which is an invaluable treasure-house for them. How to use that treasure-house while teaching is an art? The teacher thus speeds up the teaching-learning process extending its advantages to the learners i.e. the students. Teaching output of a teacher is appraised when the students are put to tests. The more the scores the better is teacher's performance. It shows the significance of tests and examinations in teaching which needs no elaboration as it is well known in the society. Appraisal of quality of teaching thus aims at its applicability and utility to teaching objectives and conformity to pre-determined standardized goals.

Teachers' performance appraisal is so far carried out with these objectives and standardized goals in mind. Its accuracy, applicability and effectiveness could be gauzed by "Student Rating Questionnaire" which is quite often criticised. Ramsden (1992) too is not happy with this proposition. Commenting on its shortcomings, he says that "Student Rating Scale" is unreliable from statistical angles. The scores and students' actual scholarly abilities do not match many a time. Therefore these are unrealistic. These "conflate stylistic and quality measures" and "equate collection of student ratings for personal purposes with their use for diagnostic feedback purposes" and will at the end "trivialize the process of improvement, damage morale, and lead to a distortion of the educational system." Instead of being qualitative it is more quantitative to please everyone.

> **Reflective Practitioner Perspective:**

It attempts to achieve the morals of education while practicing teaching. It is a complex process. These morals can be expressed in dictums of educational belief and values. Practice is insignificant in this perspective because of the belief that such values are inherent in a teaching practitioner who can be refined by training and practice. Exponents of this perspective say that a good performance "is one which calls forth abilities that are critical for success in the given context" (Bridges et al. 1986).

The professional knowledge is the offspring of memory of past experience and working-culture. According to Elliot (1988) they have the capacity of retaining the creative thoughts and ideas which could be utilized to find solutions to the problems. Eraut (1992) says these structures may be of three kinds: Propositional, Personal and Process knowledge." The third is very important with reference to professional performance because it consists of five kinds of processes: Acquiring knowledge, Skilled behaviour, Deliberative processes, Passing on information and Controlling own behaviour.

Holistically, the professional knowledge means recalling those skills stored in the memory which could be utilized in particular situations to achieve those objectives which are value based. This effort is complex so as to give a concrete shape to those ideas because until the ideas and the ideals are given a solid shape, they cannot be used. They ought to be used practically; even if such activities are also temporary and hypothetical. Still deliberations on the objectives and their practice could be done only in those situations in which they occur. Reflections and the practice based on that could be justified with reference to the objectives of this exercise which are: Utility of exercise, its objectives, setting those objectives, basis for reforms, students who become motivators for all these and the references in which these activities take place. This is the individual commitment which is associated with professional values and the analytical approach which speeds up reformation process and creates such situations in which opportunities and constraints are likely to emerge more and more. Thus this exercise/practice is internally motivated and externally activated.

Teaching is not only formal and well-regulated transmission of knowledge but certainly more than that; and that is an exhortation to analytical learning by both: The teacher and the taught; and thereafter extending the maximum support for it. The problems that crop up during this practice is that that they may be unique and challenging because they emerge from unexpected situations for which both of them are unprepared. These could be entirely new: Formerly not encountered either by the teacher or by the student. These obstacles set the limits of the teacher's academic knowledge and professional experience. Irrelevant and incoherent text could be made clear by the actions and reactions of the teacher. The general hypotheses that are formed on the basis of past experiences could be tackled by the teacher's intelligent interpretations. Problem solving involves not only following specific procedures but also self-knowledge, its proper and relevant use, prompt decision-making skills and a keen insight into which techniques should be used. And all this requires an autonomy which is envisaged by the reflective practitioner's perspective. Gaining professional knowledge and its practice are interdependent and are complementary to each other. Therefore, learning, practice and innovations interplay with each other. They sustain jointly. It is this research aptitude which reflects the internal prowess of an individual and brings them to the fore. The fact of the matter is that the whole exercise is a combination of art and research which ignites the internal appetite of students and the teachers equally and exhibits their capabilities for it. According to Ramsden (1987) quality, in this perspective, "is not about performing well to please one's (superiors); still less is it about fulfilling criteria imposed by administrative agencies. It is an outcome of a duty towards oneself to be excellent" with reference to values of practice.

In this perspective, all problems, difficulties and complexities are to be identified together. It takes special care to the suitable techniques which could be used to achieve the best and maximum result by using professional and academic knowledge gained from various resources for self-learning and self-monitoring. Managerial objectives have no place in this perspective. Undoubtedly there are some objectives in this perspective too but they are not result-oriented because the objectives being hypothetical could never be forecast whether they will be proved or not. Yes, development: Professional and institutional are sure to take place benefits of which ultimately go in favour of the organisations. Therefore, freedom to take decisions goes a long way in achieving even the hypothetical objectives in creative manner.

A hundred dollar question is whether the "Technical Perspective" "Reflective Perspective" and the "Reflective Practitioner Perspective" could be separated? The issue may be academically debated upon but in practice, it is not possible at all. Reasons are obvious. Reflections are also made and directed on the basis of pre-determined values, past knowledge and already acquired skills. The "Technical Perspective" thus is a launching pad for the "Reflective Perspective" and the "Reflective Practitioner Perspective." And why do those who look at them as separate entities, forget the fact that today's "Reflective Practitioner Perspective" will be "Technical Perspective" tomorrow. Every research or innovation is a part of the long chain of "Reflective Practitioner Perspective." Even if a single part of the chain goes missing, the whole is lost. The researches and innovations are made in a chain of investigative events and their relevance depends on its continuity. Therefore, whatever the perspective is; its objective is one: And that is professional growth of the individual and all-round development of the organisation. Both exist or die together. None has an independent existence. Therefore, while appraising teaching performance, the appraisers must keep these aspects in mind to ensure growth and development in totality.

All-round development can be possible only when the institutional rules, its objectives, employees' professional goals, their knowledge, experience and the urge for innovations are in sync with each other. Such scenario will ensure all-round individual growth and institutional development.

❑❑❑❑

CHAPTER 5

Teachers' Appraisal Procedures

Our personal view and experience is if we have to mentally prepare the teachers for teaching performance appraisal, we must train them in self-appraisal first and then go for their performance appraisal. As pointed out earlier also that monthly self-appraisal could be very useful. If the institutions/organisations wish both: Self-appraisal and performance appraisals can run together. There is no harm in it only if the teachers and appraisers can bear the burden of both. The institutions and the appraisers should not forget that the training in self-appraisal has also to be imparted to the teachers by them.

5.1   Analytical Review of Self-appraisal:

It has been discussed in brief in earlier Chapter two as well. But being very significant in appraisal-systems, it needs further deep analysis. Self-appraisal means evaluating the quality of one's own performance. The teacher or any other worker analyses his own work and conduct under this scheme and identifies his/her shortcomings so as to overcome them for further improvement. She/he also looks at her/his strengths and tries to judge their impact on her/his work in order to strengthen them according to needs. If explained in other words, appraiser and the appraisee are both rolled into one: That is the teacher or employee who assesses the utility or disutility of his performance and tries to improve the performance wherever need is felt or modifies her/his strategies if found to be unfit. The art of Self-appraisal is not easy to adopt just because finding fault with self or one's own performance is too difficult to be implemented. But if adopted honestly, self-appraisal has several advantages. Self-appraisal has many advantages which may prove to be mile-stones in the tedious journey of self-improvement and development.

> **Advantages of Self-appraisal:**

a. Self-appraisal encourages for self-diagnosis.
b. Self-appraisal facilitates self-treatment as well.
c. Keeps one ever alert to self-conduct.
d. Boosts up self-confidence.
e. Highlights the importance for performance appraisal.
f. Self-appraisal encourages teachers to invite and honour feedback from the students as there is no other source for it.
g. It develops the self-analytical faculties.
h. It makes the self-appraiser accountable to self.
i. It prepares the teachers for performance appraisals.

5.2 Prior Steps for Self appraisal:

a. The teacher sets the objectives for his self-appraisal which may be as follows:

   i. Decides which lessons or units have to be taught during the month.
   ii. Chooses concept-related humorous anecdotes to make the teaching interesting.
   iii. Decides which concepts to be written and highlighted on the blackboard.
   iv. Chooses and practises body language appropriate to the lesson thus preparing her/him for role-play.
   v. Weekly distribution of the lessons for convenient handling.
   vi. Decides daily home-work to be given to the students.

b. The points to be taken care of for classroom management:

   i. Where and how he will keep an eye in the class while teaching.
   ii. Where and when he will move in the class during teaching.
   iii. Which weak students he will pay more attention.
   iv. How to communicate with the students.
   v. Which testing or probing questions he will put during teaching.
   vi. How to get additional feedback from the students?
   vii. Any other point that he may deem fit and appropriate.

5.3   Students for Feedback on Teaching:

The teachers get a lot of feedback automatically from the students when they communicate with them during teaching, even then to get it from students on different aspects of his teaching he will have to invite and encourage them to express their views, opinions and suggestions freely and without any fear or favour. This is essential because the students quite often hesitate to express themselves especially when they are asked to speak about their teachers. Main reasons for this are:

i.   One, the traditional respect for the teachers. It is a good tradition. The teachers ought to be respected. But the teachers should be more open-minded with their students especially to know about their professional acumen. They should make two things very clear to their students. One, their teaching being student-centered, must be rated by them as its beneficiaries and that they should not hesitate at all to tell how much they gained from their teaching style. Was their voice audible to the last bencher or not and was it comprehensible or incomprehensible? Second, giving opinion to the teacher respectfully is a healthy sign of good relations between the teachers and the students. It is not bad if the students express their difficulties in understanding any concept. The teacher must make it amply clear that he would welcome his students' opinions or suggestions so that he could make more efforts in making his teaching effective. If the teacher develops such a cordial rapport with his students that they never hesitate in expressing themselves before him, it will be an extra feather in the cap of the teacher.

ii.   Second, most of the students fear their teachers, especially those who bear grim faces and feel disgraceful or inappropriate to smile before their students. The teachers' notion that by keeping grim faces they can keep their students disciplined is absolutely wrong. To be serious and to be serious with work are entirely different things. The latter is a good sign because it improves the work culture of the class but the former is bad because it increases an unnatural distance between the teachers and students and creates undesired fear or hesitation among the students. The students hesitate to put even the genuine questions related to the topic being taught. So the teachers should always try to fill this gap between them and their students to facilitate smooth and uninterrupted communication which is essential for good teaching. This they can do it just by improving their Sense of Humour which will certainly brighten up their faces and encourage their students to put genuine questions before them.

5.4   Significance of Students' Feedback:

Appraisal whether done by self or any other person, is useless and meaningless until its results which in human resource terms is called the feedback, is adequately provided to the appraisee. The renowned writer and management expert Kenneth Blanchard says that feedback is the breakfast of the champions of their field. Regular feedback strengthens an individual's performance and enhances his/her personal and professional development. For a leader, his/her team is the best source of feedback: positive or negative, and he/she can act upon it to improve himself/herself. Sharad Sharma, Director and Chief, HR Department, Vertax Customer Services India Pvt. Ltd. Says, "Seeking feedback from employees' works wonders for leaders who are making sincere attempts to transit from an aristocratic leadership approach to a more collaborative style. Communication is not only about speaking alone, but also listening . . . . and the leader, who demonstrates good listening skills, is more likely to be regarded highly." Similarly, Raman Subramanian, Vice President, Strategic Services Management, QuEST Global opines, "Taking feedback from the employees is one of the cornerstones of establishing a successful working relationship and creating a feeling of openness in the organisation."

"Leaders can seek anonymous/confidential feedback from their team by using tools like 360-degree feedback, circle of feedback, hot-seat feedback (a face to face controlled feedback mechanism), HPLA (High Performance Leadership Assessment), CASE (Community, Authenticity, Significance and Excitement) etc. Effective leaders can make feedback a part of their organisational culture and seek non-anonymous feedback using similar tools," says Ashish Arora, Founder and MD, HR Anexi.

Anonymous feedback could be more realistic because the unrevealed identity of the feedback provider gives him freedom to express. Teachers could use this technique on their students as well to get the realistic feedback. Whatever is the form of feedback i.e. anonymous or otherwise, the appraisee should never be judgmental or subjective; rather he should utilize this opportunity to learn more about his way of working and what others feel about it; and should try to modify it wherever it is felt necessary. Ashish Arora, Founder and Managing Director H.R. Anexi further says, "Receive feedback with gratitude and never shoot the messenger. Take feedback just as you receive a gift from someone you respect; even if it is not pleasant, say "Thank You."

5.5   Forms of Teachers' Appraisal:

We shall appreciate if we remind the readers that an impartial and up to mark performance appraisal has an equal and total effect on the employees as well as the organisations. May we prepare the forms of teachers' performance appraisal, but they cannot be separated because their objectives are the same. If the teachers are aware of their responsibilities, will the students and the institutions not get full benefits of it? In the same way, if professional development takes place, will the teachers' personal and individual development remain behind? As far as the appraisal made by a supervisor is concerned, its kinds based on their objectives could be of three types. They are Accountability Centric Appraisal, Profession Centric Appraisal and the Employee Centric Appraisal.

5.6   Accountability Centric Appraisal:

a.   **Qualities:**

   i.   It makes the teachers accountable. Accountability could be individual as well as collective.
   ii. The appraiser is normally a senior who is not only aware of his responsibilities but also makes his subordinates accountable to them.
   iii. It unifies the appraisal area, appraisal rules and appraisal forms to facilitate accurate appraisal.

iv. Appraisal results are used to improve performance, promotions, and man-management; and to settle other administrative matters.

v. The performance is shown in grades to eliminate doubts.

vi. Employees' responsibilities are expressed clearly so that the employee has no doubts about his job and he does it with accuracy.

b. Procedure:

i. The appraiser meets the appraisee in the beginning of the session and finalizes the area for appraisal.

ii. The area of appraisal is decided according to the responsibilities of the teacher.

iii. The appraiser collects teacher's performance data from the following resources:

  a. From students' exercise books.
  b. From progress reports of the students.
  c. From teaching supervision.
  d. From home work management.
  e. From the quality of home checking.
  f. From examination papers set by the appraisee.
  g. From examination answer sheets' checking.
  h. From weekly/monthly test papers.
  i. From teachers' diary.
  j. From other co-curricular activities/organised and academic works performed by the appraisee.
  k. From other relevant records.

c. Post-appraisal interaction:

i. The appraiser and the appraisee meet to discuss appraisal issues.

ii. Appraisal area decided with mutual understanding and with the appraisees' consent.

iii. Performance appraisal criteria discussed.

iv. Feedback according to the output of the appraisal assured.

v. Appreciation of good performance assured.

   vi. Suggestions extended for good performance.

   vii. In case of performance below expectations, advisories will be given and suggestions will be made for improvement.

   viii. Preparing the performance appraisal reports with mutual discussions. Both will approve it.

   ix. Feedback will be monitored.

   x. One copy of the appraisal report will be given to the teacher.

d.   Conclusion:

   i. If the teacher still has any grievances, both review the appraisal report.

   ii. If the differences remain unresolved, the chief reviews the report and takes necessary action.

   iii. If the issue still persists, the grievance redressal committee reviews the report. The teacher is given an opportunity to put up his case so that the differences are removed in a cordial atmosphere. At this stage, the decision taken is final.

5.7   Professional Centric Appraisal:

a.   Qualities:

   i. Emphasizes professional development.

   ii. Normally the appraisal is done by an expert. He may not be a senior.

   iii. Appraisal areas are mutually decided.

   iv. Appraisal report is flexible. Open for free discussion.

   v. Rules of appraisal mutually discussed and decided.

   vi. Minimum use of grades.

   vii. Most of the feedback is narrative and explained thoroughly.

b.   Procedure:

   i. Pre-appraisal discussions. Appraiser and the appraisee meet to mutually decide the appraisal areas.

   ii. Data for appraisal is collected from the following resources:

      a. From students' exercise books.

      b. From students' progress reports.

   c.   From performance appraisal.

   d.   From home work management.

   e.   From home work checking.

   f.   From question papers set by the appraisee.

   g.   From examination answer books.

   h.   From appraisees' diary.

   i.   From other works/duties performed by the teacher/appraisee.

   k.   From other relevant records.

c.   Post-appraisal Interaction

   i.   The appraiser and the appraisee meet to discuss appraisal results mutually.

   ii.   Areas of good performance are identified and appreciated.

   iii.   Feedback is provided for improvement.

   iv.   Both, the appraiser and the appraisee make the best use of the appraisal.

   v.   Both prepare a plan for further improvement.

   vi.   Both decide how to implement the improvement plan so as to ensure professional development of the appraisee.

   vii.   In the light of the feedback given to the appraisee he makes his views clear how he would facilitate institutional development in future.

   viii.   Keeping the above points in (v) to (vii) in view, appraisal report is prepared with mutual consent.

   ix.   Both sign the report.

   x.   Recommendations are also executed earnestly.

d.   Conclusion:

   i.   If need arises, the report is reviewed and the teacher's grievances are listened.

   ii.   If grievances remain unresolved, the report is reviewed by the grievance redressal committee.

   iii.   The teacher is given an opportunity to put up his case.

   iv.   If the issues remain still unresolved, the Head reviews the report and takes a final decision which ought to be acceptable to all.

5.8   Employee Centric Appraisal:

As the name suggests, its aim is development of the employees/ teachers. But an important question that comes to mind is whether only individual development in any institution/organisation is possible i.e. without leaving other areas uninfluenced by this development. Even if we agree that a management may be so liberal and open-hearted that it aims at only the individuals' professional development leaving other areas untouched, then the question again crops up if this development, may be individual, will not affect the whole organisation in the long run. Truth is that any kind of development will ultimately benefit all: The employees/teachers, institutions, students, parents and ultimately the whole society. We cannot segregate one development from the other. That is why Accountability Centric Appraisal and Profession Centric Appraisal have been considered to be the best which have been discussed in detail above.

5.9   Critical Analysis of Performance Appraisal Practices:

All the practices used for performance appraisal are criticised on one pretext or the other. Though widely criticised but the truth is that there is no shortcoming in either of the practices. If there are any discrepancies, those are due to their wrong use by untrained people or due to subjective attitude of the appraisers or drifting away from the appraisal areas. There is no basis for their uncalled for criticism. If these are used properly, these could be termed as the best. The criticism generally focuses on the following points:

i.   Influence of subjectivity:

Lack of objectivity is the main grouse of the critics. They say that the appraiser has too much freedom and he becomes too subjective. The argument is sound because the appraiser too is a human-being with weaknesses of likes and dislikes which may affect the appraisal process. Very few appraisers escape such weaknesses. Instead of looking at the work-performance of the appraisee they start evaluating the person. The appraisees who perfect in the art of flattering the appraiser often get more or better grades. Just opposite to this are those employees who are good performers but poor at flattering. It is also a universally accepted fact that good performers do not like flattery. Though they work sincerely with their zeal even then such employees are often at a loss if the appraiser is not objective. It is also generally seen that the flatterers are shirkers and do not sincerely work because they have confidence over their art of flattery and they spend their time and energy in pleasing the seniors. Under such circumstances, the onus of quality appraisal falls fully on the appraiser. If he is good appraiser, he will have to give his attention more to the teacher's work instead of his personality. He should appraise and rate his performance and award his work keeping his performance in view. Another objection of the critics of these practices is that these cannot appraise immeasurable performances like honesty, sincerity, commitment etc. It is true. These qualities may not be directly connected to the performance of any employee, but there is no doubt that such qualities indirectly have a great impact on the performance of an employee.

It is also true that howsoever the appraiser may try to be objective; subjectivity too creeps in quietly at times. But this allegation of subjectivity is very serious, and therefore, the appraiser has to be very cautious during the entire appraisal-process. He should pay more attention to the performance than the performer otherwise he is likely to do more injustice than justice to the employee in particular and the organisation in general. Besides harming an employee, it will certainly taint the image of the organisation also because the sincere employees hardly stay in such organisations for long. They try to leave such institutions as soon as they get a chance. Faulty appraisals are also legally challenged and if the appraisal is rejected by the statutory bodies, the organisation is defamed and therefore it has to bear the brunt.

ii. Halo Error:

This situation arises when the appraiser impressed by anyone good or bad characteristics of the performance, focuses only on it and rates it (the performance) good or bad. The appraiser should skirt such phenomenon because either the employee is unduly rewarded or punished by it. The organisation too does not gain from it in any way.

iii.   Leniency:

When the appraiser becomes too much moderate during the appraisal process and awards more grades than the appraisee deserves, he is termed to be lenient. There may be several positive or negative reasons for such approach. The notion of the appraiser that strict grading may demoralize the employee or spoil his career may be a positive reason. Sometimes, the appraisee may be under stress due to personal reasons and the appraiser comes to know about it, he may become sympathetic and gives him more marks. There is no harm in it until the appraisee is undeserving. Sometimes, the appraiser chooses to defend or conceals the bad-work-culture of the organisation; may be due to please the bosses or to seek the favour of employees or not to antagonize the tough workers or to avoid the responsibility of justifying his appraisal results if challenged. It is also often observed that the appraisers become very lenient if the appraisal is used for raise in salary or for promotions.

Appraisal process is very important not only for the employees and organisations but for the appraisers also. The latter have to discuss, analyse and review the appraisal process, results and the feedback given for further improvement with the employees and organisation heads. So the appraisers ought to keep their appraisal skills up to date lest they face any difficulty at any crucial stage. Their lenient views during appraisal process may cause several problems/wrongs which may be:

a.   What serious consequences could be due to overlooking the weaknesses of the employees during appraisal, can be visualised even by an illiterate. If the weaknesses are not pointed out in time, how will the employee professionally and individually grow?

b.   When a proficient employee sees undeserving or low-performer getting better grades, he feels demoralized which leads to fall in the work-culture of the organisation and development of inferiority complex among good employees.

c.   The appraisal records are used for many purposes in which includes raise in salaries, promotions, giving other benefits to the employees and even demotions. If the employees are appraised leniently, then the ineligible will be rewarded and the eligible may be left out due to meager resources. If it so happens, the organisation will be tight-fisted in rewarding even the deserving employees. Promotions and raise in salaries will have to be curtailed. Such situation can never be appreciated. In the absence of motivators, even the best of employees will feel demoralized and the whole of the organisation will suffer.

d. The fall out of lenient appraisal is clearly startling when the organisation wants to get rid of an average performer who was judged as good before. In such cases, it becomes a herculean task to sack such an employee just because the entire past appraisal records are in his favour.

iv.   Strictness:

Just opposite to lenient is the strict appraisal. This attitude could also be not called healthy. If the former may reward undeserving, the latter may punish even a good performer just because of the strict attitude of the appraiser. It may be due to strict rules of the appraiser or due to strict implementation of the appraisal procedures or appraiser's poor understanding of these procedures. Sometimes strictness is used to motivate the employees to work harder in future or to bring the disobedient/careless/poor-performers to book. Thus strict appraisal is used as a remedy to cure an ailment of indiscipline and poor performance. But such tricks do not work well always. Sometime, they may boomerang.

Strict appraisal may be useful if it is uniform throughout and all appraisers are equally strict. In other words, there should be one yardstick for all. But it does not happen so always. Its purpose will be lost if one appraiser is strict and the other is lenient. A good performer will always be at loss if he is appraised by a strict appraiser as compared to a low performer but appraised by a lenient appraiser. Such situations could never be favourable for any one: Employee as well as the organisation just because it will spoil the cordial atmosphere of the organisation. Such appraisal may demoralize even the good performers which certainly will be counter-productive because both: Employee and the organisation cannot remain unaffected by this approach. Strict appraisal creates a scaring atmosphere in the organisation. And a scared work force can never be at ease. So such an atmosphere will be detrimental to healthy individual growth and professional development. Due to reasons given in 'c' and 'd' above, the appraisee will never feel free to participate in pre-appraisal discussions or post-appraisal analyses and the very purpose of the appraisal exercise will be defeated. The employees in such a scenario, start shirking work. When they see undeserving being rewarded, the good employees also start following the same course and the healthy-work-culture of the organisation is badly hurt.

v.   **Central Tendency:**

This error occurs when the appraiser rates an appraisee in the middle of the scale. In other words, the appraisee is judged as an average performer. This may happen on two counts. One, the appraiser is ill-trained in the use of the rating scale. Two, he is ill-equipped to defend his appraisal conclusions. So in order to avoid post-appraisal controversies, he chooses the safest way of awarding average category to the appraisee. Its effects will also be adverse as in the case of lenient or strict appraisal.

vi.   **Influenced by Hypocritical Behaviour:**

Sometimes it so happens that the appraisees artificially change their behaviour around the appraisal time and pose to be very polite, docile, obedient, committed, punctual and diligent. It is just like camouflaging self to dodge the enemy in war. Here is this case the appraisee dodge the observer. It is an attempt to hide the reality. Such changes are more observed in the stubborn employees. The appraiser, who is unknown to the reality, is easily influenced by such fake behaviour and puts the appraisee on a high pedestal for which he never deserves. But the appraiser should never be influenced by the general behaviour of the appraisee and always keep the area of appraisal in mind and should not stray beyond that.

vii. Bias:

Sometimes, the appraiser gets personal due to caste, colour, creed or sex of the appraisee and lets the appraisal affected by such personal views. We may find such bias in armed forces or police departments also where the women employees are not appraised on the same level as their male counterparts. This type of bias is absolutely unjustified. Appraisal standards do not permit such discriminations. Such discriminations are against law too. But truth is that such favoritism still exists. Consequently, good performers get punished and low-performers get rewarded. If the teacher/worker is hostile and tough, she/he is rated good either out of fear or to avoid post-appraisal confrontations. Similarly a soft-spoken good performer does not get what he deserves. The appraisers should steer clear of such situations because they may create grave problems leading to agitations in the organisations.

viii. Judgmental Attitudes of the Appraiser:

It is also seen quite often that the appraisers shower favours on undeserving employees due to extraneous reasons like flattery they relish or the gifts they receive from the appraisees. Women employees are not only discriminated due to their sex, but are also harassed for sexual favours. Such news or charges are quite common; which may be a bit exaggerated but are not fully untrue. Such favours are commonly heard when annual increments are given or promotions are made. This phenomenon not only creates ill-will among the employees but also brings a bad name to the whole organisation.

ix. Unrealisric Appraisal:

Another faulty tendency is seen when the appraisers appraise the employees in an unrealistic manner. The employee actually performs well but the appraiser due to reasons best known to him, gives the appraisee poor grades. It may be due to his personal likes and dislikes; or on account of pressure from the management. This tendency can never be useful for anyone: The employee, the organisation and even the appraiser. So it must be dropped.

x.   Absence of Timely Feedback:

The appraisers sometimes commit a grievous mistake by avoiding giving feedback immediately after the appraisal. It may be due to several reasons. Not able to make appraisal notes simultaneously while doing appraisal, being biased with the appraisee, due to unrealistic appraisal or appraiser lacking self-confidence etc. maybe the causes for delay in giving the feedback. This is a grave lapse. Appraisal without timely feedback is just like diagnosing the patient without prescribing treatment for the recovery. The appraiser has to be extra cautious and alert in preparing the feedback and in giving it just after the appraisal otherwise the whole purpose will be lost.

xi.   Incapabilities of the Appraiser:

Sometimes the appraiser is so inexperienced and incompetent that he fails to identify the weak areas where the appraisee should pay more attention for improvement in performance. In such circumstances, how can he possibly prepare his appraisal report? Neither he will be able to give any feedback to the appraisee nor any suggestion to the organisation for development with reference to the appraisal. The appraisers ought to be fully trained in appraisal work and must have deep knowledge and experience of this responsible job and overcome all his incapability.

So far, one thing is crystal clear that the fault lies not in appraisal practices but in their use by incompetent, inexperienced and biased appraisers. If the appraisers are well-trained, highly experienced and absolutely objective, there is no reason to say that the practice/s is/ are faulty. Need is for the appraisers to come clean while performing the appraisal work. If they do not and start blaming the practices, then they will just be like bad workmen quarrelling with their tools. They should avoid such situations because in it lies the good of the employees, organisations and them too.

5.10   Diagnosis of Appraisal Errors:

It is certain that some mistakes are committed intentionally or unintentionally by the appraisers while doing this serious work.

Therefore it becomes necessary that steps to avoid such mistakes must be taken. If the following measures are taken in earnest, some kind of check may be applied against such lacunas to a great extent:

i.   Try to be as objective as possible. It will altogether reduce chances of committing any appraisal error.
ii. If any error occurs even after that prepare a correct description of the lacuna.
iii. Find out the causes of such an occurrence even after precautions.
iv. Highlight the significance of the lacuna.
v.   Judge if the lacuna is due to personal inefficiencies or due to any other reason.
vi. Appraise the appraiser to judge whether he is trained in art of appraising.
vii. Ensure that all the necessary practical or otherwise preparations have been made before the appraisal procedure begins.
viii. Find out whether the appraiser was unbiased and impartial with the appraisee.

5.11   Conclusion:

According to the experience of the human resource management experts, the best system could be that which facilitates the professional progress of any working group and meets their professional and personal needs. By adopting such a system, we can ensure quality education, teachers' professional development and their individual growth. After studying above procedures, one thing is quite clear that the appraisal system of any institution decides its ideals, values and the management structure.

Sometimes performance appraisal systems get inter-mingled due to complex and unbelievable situations. It affects the teachers' expectations and their receptive prowess to such an extent that the organisation has to automatically find its own appraisal system which may achieve its specific objectives. Where quality and development are important as specific goals, it should also be ensured that all organisational traditions, customs and procedures aim at meeting the expectations of the teachers. It will help in understanding the organisation in its totality, its employees and their work-culture.

The discipline that is needed for achieving institutional objectives is established by the performance appraisal system of that institution. It also motivates the teachers to continue updating their teaching skills to ensure quality teaching. One thing needs to be kept in mind. Where the productivity is judged in terms of its cost and analytical qualities are overlooked, the contributions of the employees and roles of the institution are of no importance. Therefore, all organisations need to promote their employees' work-interests, their duties to be specified clearly, show interest in educational schemes and never hesitate in boosting up their morale so as to integrate productivity and its costs with reference to the institution and its manpower. Only then the institutional goals could be achieved.

Mere keeping inspection reports, questionnaires and schemes which do not aim at teachers' professional development, do no good even to the institutions. When these tools are arranged and used in such a way that they motivate the teachers to such an extent that they compete with each other to achieve rarest of the rare resources, then not only the teachers professional growth speeds up but it also ensure institutional growth and excellent work-culture based on collaboration among all.

Through pre-appraisal discussions (some call them interviews); teachers' special capabilities are easily recognised. It gives them their own identity. Effective teaching techniques encourage the teachers to do better. The teachers' healthy attitudes and will-power are revealed in a positive manner. If pre-appraisal discussions are held with reference to the pre-determined goals, it shows the autocratic tendencies of the management. Discussions are necessary for quality and further development. Therefore they should not be bound by any limitations like that of pre-determined goals. Collaboration is not only necessary for quality management but also for the whole organisation. Management is not only to command or to supervise the employees. It is also for listening to the problems of its employees and understanding their expectations from the institution. Only this type of positive attitude will do well to not only the employees but the institutions also.

❑❑❑❑

CHAPTER 6
Need-based Performance Appraisal

Every institution, organisation and industry requires need-based appraisal system so that its goals and objectives could be thoroughly understood and achieved. But the education sector needs it the most. The reasons are obvious. Every institution is unique in its character which is greatly influenced by the domestic, social, economic and psychological background of the teachers, the taught and even other staff members irrespective of their roles in the institution. All the objectives of the institution are set and educational planning is done by keeping all these factors in mind. Therefore it is necessary as well as timely that the educational institutions are given the liberty to hold need-based-performance appraisals. It will not only ensure maximum use of the available resources and but also be very useful for the students. Therefore the need-based-performance appraisal will have to be necessarily allowed in order to make the best use of the available resources to extend maximum benefit to the students/ learners and to provide them quality education. What after all are the goals of any educational institutions? That is the development of their infrastructure so as to meet immediate needs of the teachers and students and to motivate the teachers and the students to achieve more than that which they have already achieved. For this the educational institutions will have to set their goals keeping these needs of the teachers and the taught, make students and teacher centric policies and adopt a need-based-performance appraisal system otherwise the institutions will certainly lag behind in achieving their goals.

Most important factors of the need-based-performance appraisal system in education are its manpower-policies with reference to its students which are to be necessarily used during the appraisal process. It is a reality that educational institutions have started performance appraisal systems but they are mostly without the real objectives. It may be to appraise teachers' capabilities or for to motivate them for doing better or for institutional development. But the real beneficiaries i.e. the students are always overlooked in this process. It is a truth though very bitter one.

What after all the educational institutions are meant for? And what after all is the duty of the teachers? Undoubtedly, the answer to both these questions is that it is the transmission of new knowledge to the students, to let them know what they do not know, to take them from known to unknown and to take them out of darkness so as to provide light: The light of knowledge. The teacher has to do this up to the entire satisfaction of the students and the educational institutions to facilitate this process their teachers are engaged in. In order to achieve this objective, they will have to plan and design the teaching-learning process in such a way that the students benefit from it the most. The teachers will also have to hone up their teaching skills, always keep the students' interests in their mind and be fully dutiful to their students. Only then they will be able to meet the expectations of their students and the institutions. For meeting these demands on the part of the students and the institutions only such appraisal systems will be successful which aim at these institutional objectives and the students' needs. These objective oriented appraisal schemes will keep them alert to the educational and students' development and will also appraise the teachers whether their performance was up to mark or not.

After deciding in favour of the need-based appraisal system, it is of top-most priority to decide the institutional objectives and to make the teachers aware of them so that they could feel accountable for the achievement of set goals. Only then the appraisal scheme could be decided what form it should take and what procedures it ought to adopt. The appraisal system of each institution has to be different suitable to its needs as it is very true that each institution is has its own character and different work-culture often shaped by the background of the teachers and the taught. Therefore it is absolutely essential that the institutional policy makers first study the background of the teachers and the taught, their work-culture and objectives of the institution thoroughly before deciding the appraisal technique and its procedures.

6.1 Goals of Need-based Performance Appraisal:

There is no need perhaps to tell what performance-appraisal means. Since it works for the personal/professional development of the appraisees and the institutional growth equally and simultaneously, its objectives will also be influenced equally by both. The Manager, Human Resource Department is responsible for its management including training and development. They get the most out of the Need-based-Appraisal. In their opinion, Need-based-appraisal has the following objectives: —

6.2 Managerial Goals:

i. Need based recruitments.
ii. Motivate the present workforce.
iii. Ensure professional development of the present workforce.

    a. To arrange on-job-training, workshops, symposiums etc.
    b. Reward the good performers in time through promotions, suitable placements within the organisation and special increments.

6.3 Performance-Appraisal Goals:

i. Supervision of and guidance to employees with collaborative spirits.
ii. Collective analysis of the appraisal results.
iii. Discard ineffective appraisal system and ensure effective management and making an environment motivated by self-discipline.

6.4 General Goals:

i. Fixing Accountability:

    a. Setting of goals through mutual discussions and review them with the same attitudes.

    (i) To set standards for providing quality education.
    (ii) To compare actual performance in the light of the standards.

(iii) To encourage and promote good performance and dutifulness.

(iv) To take necessary steps to improve average performance through proper guidance, by attaching the low-performer with a senior expert or by issuing cautionary notes etc.

b. Staff Motivation:

(i)   By recognizing the teachers' good work.

(ii) By providing quality training.

(iii) By providing creative feedback.

c. Professional Development:

(i)   Helping the teachers in recognizing their talents and skills and improve them further to ensure institutional total development.

(ii) Helping those teachers who fail to come up to desired standards.

(iii) Whenever a situation demands, the teachers should be sponsored for special training or courses.

(iv) By apprising everyone about the infrastructural developmental steps taken so that all the teachers could put the available resources to the best use.

6.5   Need-based Appraisal Procedures:

The institutions ought to keep their objectives in mind while choosing the kind of appraisal system. The other aspects that require attention before making a choice are: —

i.   First of all the appraisal period should be decided. Whether it should be half-yearly or yearly, should be mutually settled and told to all. Newly appointed teachers ought to be appraised quarterly or half yearly whereas the old ones may be after every two years.

ii. It should also be decided whether all the teachers will be appraised every time or a few selected ones. Our opinion about this is the same i.e. as in (i) above. More and special attention is needed for new recruits. Old and experienced could appraise the new ones which will professionally help them as well.

6.6   Principles of Appraisal:

i.   What principles to be followed during appraisal ought to be made amply clear?

ii.   Transparency and objectivity must be maintained at all costs.

iii. Everyone ought to be very clear what is expected of him.

iv.   Principles and key points of appraisal should be decided collectively and with mutual consent.

v.   Key points serve as guiding tools for the appraisal which may be influenced by time, ground-realities and place. Therefore the appraisers ought to revise them from time to time and as per need.

vi.   The principles and key-points cannot be same for all: The new teachers and old ones. Therefore their separate sets ought to be prepared for both.

vii. The principles and key-points could differ from subject to subject and working areas. Therefore these factors ought to be kept in mind when deciding them.

viii. The principles and key-points should be related to teaching work only. Subjectivity of the appraiser should never creep into the appraisal system. Nor any other work unrelated to teaching should be included in appraisal.

ix.   The principles and key-points should be related to objectives too. For example: —

   a. If the appraisal is to appraise accountability and total performance of the teacher, then the grading scale should be used profusely so that the teacher could know his position well. He should remain in no doubts about his performance.

   b. If the appraisal is to appraise developmental aspects, then analytical notes should be used profusely so that the weaker areas could be highlighted in comprehensible terms.

6.7   Selection of Appraisers:

Selection procedures for the appraisers that are commonly used by the educational institutions are based on objectives. If the appraisal is for fixing the accountability of the teacher then appraiser ought to be senior to the appraisee. These could be: —

a. In education institutions, the Principal or the Vice Principal quite often works as appraisers. Since they are experienced educators, their appraisal is considered trustworthy.
b. For professional development the appraisers are chosen from the field experts. If the emphasis of the appraisal is on teaching, then he should be an educationist. If the emphasis is on any other aspect, then the expert of that field needs to be selected for reliable appraisal.
c. If the emphasis is on teaching-skills then the experts of teaching-skills are selected who does the appraisal and then suggest ways for improvement through their model teaching.
d. Sometimes, the educational institutions select a group of experts of different fields for appraisal.
e. For objective and realistic appraisal, the institutions sometimes engage appraisers from outside also. The idea behind this is that an insider may become biased with the appraisee and an outsider being unknown to him, will be stay impartial.

6.8   Appraisal Preparations:

Among the appraisal systems, appraisal procedures, pre-appraisal discussions and how their records/data are to be prepared and kept are included. But these systems will be of no utility until the appraisees are well-acquainted with them. Therefore, in order to make the best use of these appraisal practices and systems, the educational institutions ought to necessarily properly educate their teachers about them. All the steps of appraisal through which the appraisees have to pass, need to be introduced.

i. The teachers should be educated about the steps and uses of appraisal through seminars, workshops and symposiums.

ii. The teachers should be well-briefed how the appraisal schemes, pro forma are to be prepared and how they are to be implemented?

iii. Teachers should be consulted about the performance-appraisal system so as to win their confidence.

iv. Invite teachers' suggestions and arrange a pre-appraisal training programme for them.

v. Teachers' Performance appraisal scheme ought to be tried through the teachers and get appraised by each other.

vi. Get the appraisal report prepared by the teachers, arrange analytical discussions and get feedback reports prepared.

vii. Let them give the feedback to the fellow-appraisees and discuss it with them.

viii. Let them make amendments to the appraisal scheme if need arises.

ix. All these steps will not only train the teachers in facing the appraisal exercises confidently but also in the art of appraisal also.

These steps are very necessary before starting the actual appraisal of teachers' performance. It will help them understand the nuances and needs of appraisal management thus minimizing several of the difficulties of the Managers. As regards the performance appraisal techniques these could be: —

i. **Self-Appraisal:** We have already dealt this topic thoroughly in Chapter two and five. Here we will like to reiterate that it is the best type of appraisal provided the teacher is well trained in this art and is honest with himself and his performance.

ii. **Peer Appraisal:** In this technique the teachers appraise each other. Being based on peer collaboration, it is very effective. It increases their self-confidence. The teachers learn a lot by observing each other. They ought to take the following measures for the success of this technique:

   a. The peer-appraisee ought to brief his peer-appraiser beforehand about his work plan and his objectives.

   b. Appraisal report and appraisal points should be prepared under the supervision of appraisal-experts and institutional objectives.

c. The peer-appraiser should act promptly in discussing the appraisal results and giving the feedback. But the following points to be specially kept in mind:

(i)   The discussion should focus on teaching only.
(ii) The discussion should not be confined to one technique only. It should consider other options also.
(iii) The teachers being peers of each other should stay free from attachments and should not favour each other. The appraisal ought to be as real as possible.

iii. **Inspection:** In this technique, the appraiser inspects the teachers' work-plans, lesson-plans, given home-work and its checking, question-paper setting, answer-books evaluation etc. and collects the relevant data from this exercise. This exercise is very useful for objective and factual appraisal of the teachers' work and his attitudes towards his daily duties and the students.

iv. **Portfolio:** It is collection of data about a teacher's working. His works related to teaching, his achievements, training undertaken by him, his innovative works and research and education lab works, seminars, workshops, symposiums attended by him are taken into account to appraise his performance. This technique also gives a lot of objective/factual information about the teacher and his work.

v. **Other Channels:**
    Formal and informal talks, discussions, daily supervision, general inspection by various experts, data related to other works performed by the teacher, educational achievements and other report, rewards and remedial steps taken for students, planning and implementation of co-curricular activities are other sources through which a teacher's appraisal could be successfully carried out. These sources also provide objective information about a teacher's performance.

6.9   Appraisal Interviews:

Such discussions which some experts call "interviews" also are very useful for performance appraisals. The appraiser gets very good suggestions, ideas and other relevant information through these pre-appraisal discussions. They also create an informal atmosphere based on cordiality and collaborative spirit between the appraisers and appraisees. The appraisee and the appraiser share important information during these face to face interactions. The following points need to be taken care of when holding these discussions:

i.   The appraiser should boost up the morale of the appraisee and should specially praise his strengths. If it is performed timely, it will certainly work as elixir to the appraisee.

ii. The appraiser ought to fully understand the skills, work-style and teaching methodology of the appraisee and apprise him of their more positive and brighter sides. It will not only boost up the teacher's morale but will also help in his professional development ultimately extending its benefit to the institution.

iii. Appraiser ought to understand the appraisees' problems, expectations and feelings and respect them. It will establish a cordial environment between the Management, appraisers and appraisees.

iv. The appraiser and the appraisee should work together to identify the appraisal areas and make an analysis of its results collectively so as to reduce friction and provide speed to the process. Time bound improvements ought to be objectives of both.

v.   The subject matter of pre-appraisal discussions should be in tune with the aims and objectives of the appraisal. At least it should not be unrelated to the objectives.

vi. During the development oriented appraisals, the appraiser should keep encouraging the appraisee because this inspirational gesture goes a long way in not only developing professional skills in the appraisee and prompt him to do better but also in developing collaborative culture in the institution.

vii. The pre-appraisal discussion should be based on mutual give and take of ideas. It will assure the appraisee that the appraiser is interested in his professional development.

viii. During accountability oriented pre-appraisal discussions, the appraiser should keep appraisees' role, his contributions towards institutional growth and development, his abilities and capabilities, needs, limitations and expectations in his mind so that he could perform his important role in an objective manner. If need arises, the appraiser should take stock of the appraisees' earlier performances too which will help him study his continuous and cumulative progress. It will give a realistic picture of his capabilities and abilities.

ix. The pre-appraisal discussions should be in comprehensible language so that the appraisees could make the best use of them. As far as possible, technical terms ought to be avoided.

6.10   Appraisal Report:

This is the most important document prepared by the appraiser after the appraisal process is over. Therefore it ought to be prepared very carefully. This document gives a detailed and systematic written view of the appraiser about the appraisees' performance. The more objective and impartial it is the more useful and beneficial it will be for the institution and the appraisees. The following aspects need to be included and highlighted in it: —

i.   The appraisees' educational and professional qualifications, his relevant experience, on-job-training undergone etc. need to be recorded precisely in the report.

ii.   The role played and the duties performed by the appraisee during the appraisal term should be carefully documented in it.

iii.   All the information regarding the appraisal pro forma, lesson-supervisions and performance appraisal should be recorded in it.

iv.   All documents used during the appraisal should also be mentioned in it.

As stated earlier, the appraisal report is very important which function as a uniting force among the appraisers, appraisees and the whole organisation. Since it is a confidential document, only senior most officials of the management who are concerned with it, should have access to it. It is an effective tool in the hands of the management to understand each other in various ways: —

i.   It is a document that defines the objectives of developmental-oriented performance-appraisal improvement and guides the appraisees to move forward towards it.

ii. It helps the institutions to arrange for the need-based training programmes.

iii. It also helps the institutional managers to understand the teachers' capabilities, their teaching styles, and their commitments to individual and institutional goals. It further helps them to chalk out personnel development programmes and if any need arises, take remedial steps too.

6.11   Complaints Redressal Procedures:

As the title suggests, it is a forum that focuses on the resolution of the grievances of the appraisees. Sometimes, it so happens that in spite of all possible efforts, differences over appraisal results crop up. Therefore, all educational institutions must have a grievance redressal system and sooner it is evolved, the better for all: Teachers and the institutions. Normally the teachers get one month to represent against the appraisal report after they get it. The Grievance Redressal Committee should act fast as the patience level of an aggrieved is always low and the process causes unnecessary anxiety to the aggrieved. An anxious person can never work in a normal manner. In case of the teachers, it is more necessary because their complacency will harm the students straight.

6.12   Follow-up Actions:

Follow-up-action is two-sided. One, management centered and the other is employee centered. The management makes arrangements for the institutional infrastructure, other work facilities, opportunities for professional development etc so that the teachers do not face any difficulty in performing their duties, in their professional development and make fresh plans for institutional growth. These facilities motivate the teachers to carry out the suggestions honestly given in the feedback. They work sincerely to achieve institutional goals as well as those which they are interested in professionally. If the facilities are not given as per requirements, naturally they will feel distressed and unmotivated leading to loss to the students in general and the institution in particular. Teachers engaged in their institutional work sincerely are like valuable assets for any institution which the latter will not like to lose. So the managements must ensure:

i.   Teachers' Professional Development:

Teachers' Professional Development is ensured by those policies
which the managements make for the professional development of
the teachers. Truth is that performance appraisal too is also one of
those teacher-centric policies. These policies motivate the teachers
to perform their roles effectively and sincerely. On the other hand,
they prepare the managements to provide all the necessary facilities
in the institution to facilitate the teachers to perform well, update
their knowledge and skills by holding seminars, workshops or
on-job-training. It will enhance the teachers' working capacity.
The appraiser must look from this angle too whether the working
conditions for teaching are up to the mark or not. Thus the
developmental policies are good for all: The institutions and the
teachers.

ii.   Helps the average performer also:

As soon as the management gets to know that any teacher lags
behind the expected performance, he should be informed about his
weaknesses immediately without any delay lest the performance
further deteriorates. He must be timely informed so that he could take
desired steps for improvement. He should be told in clear terms where
he lacks, what his weak areas are and what he should do to overcome
them. If he does not come up to the desired standards even after such
guidance, the appraiser should come forward in second phase of
appraisal to assist him. These weaknesses could be in the main focus
during the second phase. If the efforts still fail to bring in desired
improvements, then there is no harm in taking disciplinary measures.
But such steps are to be taken as a last resort and that too after making
the concerned teacher realise what the management is worried about
the institution and him so that he does not feel hurt or humiliated.

iii.   Provides guidance to the institutions too:

On the basis of these appraisals, not only the teachers benefit but the
institutions also can learn a lot about whether they are doing or not
what they are supposed to do; and if not where they lag behind. Are
they maintaining such cordial relations with their employees who

they are expected to develop a collaborative work culture? Some managements use the appraisals for administrative purposes and others which believe in human values and are open-hearted use them for developmental works, give their employees maximum facilities and provide professional opportunities for further development. Whatever may be the managements' approach to the appraisals both should be extra careful in rewarding good performance and take cautionary measures against average or poor performance without wasting time.

6.13 More Follow-up-actions:

i. Arrange for on-job-training, hold seminars and workshops and motivate all the teachers to participate in them wholeheartedly.
ii. Learn and let them learn; and get inspiration from each other's performance.
iii. Let the teachers study appraisal reports carefully and get them very well acquainted with them.
iv. Get appraisal reports prepared by the teachers.
v. Let the teachers study appraisal reports and analyse follow-up steps like rewards and other disciplinary measures.
vi. Let the teachers swap their roles and perform on them; and let them have firsthand experience.
vii. Make a teachers' forum and let them participate in it actively.
viii. Let the teachers prepare programmes of institutional functions, let them conduct these programmes independently and preside over them.
ix. Let them join functions of neighbouring institutions.

6.14 More Suggestions

Though these points have been discussed off and on earlier also but their mention in brief here will be timely:

i. Teachers' performance appraisal time-table should be prepared in advance and all should be briefed about it so that everyone may be ready for it.
ii. The pre-appraisal discussions should be open. Each others' views should be welcome and discussed thoroughly. Freedom

of expression is always good. New ideas emerge from them. Even the inactive workers/teachers are seen taking deep interest if they are given opportunities to open up.

iii. Collaborative work culture should be promoted. Not only the senior teachers but even the talented junior ones ought to be engaged in planning, implementation and appraisal works. It will boost up their morale. They will feel attached to the institution. It will be beneficial for both.

❑❑❑❑

CHAPTER 7

Appraisal Discussion: Necessary Skills

Appraisal discussion is that procedure during which the appraiser and the appraisee are face to face either to gather information before appraisal or after it for providing feedback to the appraisee or the appraisee informing the appraiser about the action taken on his suggestions for improvements. These pre and post appraisal discussions which are often called interviews, have various objectives. Keeping these objectives in mind the interviewer or the initiator of the dialogue has to decide which skills to be used during these discussions. At this point an important question arises what after all the objectives of these discussions could be? These needs are decided by the problems/issues/difficulties faced by the educational institutions during their functioning for achieving their goals. Appraisal after all is made to sort out issues faced during "performance" for the "production" that is educating the students.

7.1   Stimulants for Appraisal Discussion/Interviews:

The situations that force institutions for appraisals and pre-appraisal discussions for conducting the exercise successfully are:

  i.   Self-appraise with reference to pre-established targets.
 ii.   Fixing production goals.
iii.   Apprising the teachers to quality of education they are giving.
 iv.   Advising the institution for development.
  v.   Approving good performance.
 vi.   Facilitating the professional and individual development of the teachers.
vii.   Grooming teachers for higher or specialized jobs.
viii.   Assimilation of the new teachers into the work-culture of the institution.
 ix.   Making a viable plan for need-based-development.
  x.   Facilitating development to maintain standards.

xi.   Deciding institutional and departmental promotions.
xii.   Enabling departmental and institutional research works.
xiii.   Brainstorming teachers to sort out sudden issues.
xiv.   Modernizing the institutional infrastructure
xv.   Setting up of the workshops and laboratories etc.

It is not possible at all that all these objectives could be covered under one pre-appraisal discussion. That is why the appraisal experts have suggested three options for the Face-to-Face Process. These are:

i.   Tell and Sell.
ii. Tell and Listen.
iii. Problem Solving.

First one gives good results in industry where the employees are briefed about quality of production for quick acceptance in the society. But it is not suitable for education sector. The latter two could be useful in education. In order of preference, the third: Problem Solving is the best for it.

With reference to the above, we have used the term "discussion" instead of "interview" which is more appropriate because interview smells of one's interrogation, investigation and testing knowledge whereas during pre-appraisal discussions there is no such intention. Pre-appraisal discussions aim at establishing a rapport with the appraisees to know what they have so far done, what they want to do and what they want to be appraised. There is nothing of the sort that these exercises could be called "interviews!" Keeping the aims and objectives of these exercises it is pertinent to call them "discussions" which will facilitate fast development of mutual faith, trust and confidence of the appraisers and the appraisees; and make the appraisal exercise successful. Besides the above, appraisal exercises are always prescriptive and educative for the institution as well as the individual teacher telling both which policies, rules and regulations, administrative set up, principles etc will be useful for both. These discussions decide the directions in which they (institution and the teachers) ought to move for betterment. These are like light-houses which do not let appraisal discussions go off their rails. It is the directive and prescriptive nature of the appraisal system that bring the appraiser and the appraisee closer. The process of appraisal may be flexible but it is still directive.

7.2   Face-to-Face Process: Main Features of.

i.   Tell and Sell:

a. Objective: Letting anyone know his strengths after appraising one's performance.
b. Psychological Assumptions: After knowing one's weaknesses the teacher resolves to improve.
c. Role of Interviewer: Discussion initiator as a decision maker.
d. Attitude of the Interviewer: The teacher benefits from the analytical approach of the appraiser and welcomes it.
e. Skills of Interviewer: The discussion initiator is an expert in selling skills.
f. Reactions of the teacher: Discards defensive and offensive behaviour.
g. Employer's Motivation for Change: Uses positive and negative motivators or both to add them to the job directly.
h. Possible gains: Profits ensured when the appraiser succeeds in winning the trust of the employees.
i. Risks of the Interviewer: Hesitation in making independent decisions. Face-saving tactics employed.
j. Probable Results: Maintains status quo.

ii.   Tell and Listen:

a. Objective: To communicate evaluation.
b. Psychological Assumptions: Change takes place if the people are non-resisting.
c. Role of Interviewer: Decision-maker.
d. Attitude of Interviewer: Can respect others if understands them.
e. Skills of Interviewer: Listening, reflecting and summarizing.
f. Reaction of Employee: Feeling of acceptance through defensive techniques.
g. Employer's Motivation for Change: Change welcomed. Positive incentives given.

h. Possible Gains: Employee develops trust in superiors. Success assured.
i. Risks of Interviewer: Need for change may not grow.
j. Probable Results: Interviewer may change according to the employer. Upward communication.

iii. **Problem Solving:**

i. <u>Objectives</u>: Stimulates growth and development.
ii. <u>Psychological Assumptions</u>: Free discussions of job problems improve performance.
iii. <u>Role of Interviewer:</u> As a facilitator.
iv. <u>Attitude of Interviewer:</u> Discussions lead to new ideas and interests.
v. <u>Skills of Interviewer:</u> Listening and reflecting feelings, ideas through probing questions.
vi. <u>Reactions of Employees:</u> Problem solving.
vii. <u>Employers' Motivation for Change:</u> Necessary freedom and responsibility given. Boosts up morale through intrinsic motivators.
viii. <u>Possible gains:</u> Improvement assured.
ix. <u>Risks of Interviewer:</u> Employees may not come up to his expectations.
x. <u>Probable Results:</u> All learn. Ideas pooled together. Change takes place.

7.3   Main Skills of Appraisal Discussion:

Keeping the directive nature of appraisal, the appraiser-interviewer has to hone up his skills so that he could make the best possible use of each minute. Guided by these skills, he sets his goals, plans his strategies and prepares the ground for useful discussion with the employee in a cordial atmosphere, understands his difficulties and problems and thereafter tries to resolve them. On the basis of skills, we may divide them into three: i. Pre-discussion Skills. ii. Main Discussion Skills. iii. Post-discussion Skills.

7.4   Pre-discussion Skills:

i. Deciding the objectives of the discussion after understanding the goals of the management.

ii. Surveying and analyzing the available records which include employee's dossier and other records. Collects relevant data from it which helps in objective appraisal.

iii. Mutual, personal and organisational matters of importance are identified beforehand for contemplation during the discussion lest any significant point is left out. The appraiser assures by this approach that no problem is left out.

iv. To fix time for each issue so that it could be addressed threadbare and the concerned could be advised accordingly.

v. Choosing time, place and environment suitable for the discussion. All should feel at home during this exercise.

vi. Finalize the strategy for the discussion and proceed accordingly.

7.5   Main Discussion Skills:

i. Contacts the teacher and establishes rapport with him to create a cordial atmosphere for discussion.

ii. Tries to know the subject matter, the topic and objectives of teaching them.

iii. Tries to understand teacher's feelings and emotions through his body language and responses to his questionnaire.

iv. With reference to the above, he interacts with the teacher to reach the bottom of the situation so that the discussion could be successful.

v. Compares discussion results with the dossier of the teacher and tries to see if there are any differences between both.

vi. If there are any variations between both, it is brought to the notice of all concerned to remove uncertainty immediately.

vii. Summarizes discussions whenever needed so that all participants are well familiar with the progress.

viii. Thereafter the discussion commences. This is time when all participants speak out their mind frankly to benefit from the open discussion.

ix. The appraiser puts his ideas in an assertive manner so that everyone listens to him carefully and implements diligently what he wants to. One thing to be noted here is that "assertive manner" does not mean "Aggressiveness" or "Dictatorship."

x.   The appraiser informs everyone about the conclusions of discussion.
xi.   Gives his suggestions.
xii.   The issues raised by the appraisee are sorted out.
xiii. Removes differences if any.
xiv.   Keeping the organisational hierarchy intact, reaches a mutual understanding.
xv.   Expectations, objectives and needs are redefined so that all know their roles.
xvi.   Oraganisational values are defined.
xvii. Face to face analytical review.
xviii. Gives feedback.
xix.   Provides effective leadership keeping roles of all and the entire scenario in mind.
xx.   Protects feelings and emotions of all.

7.6   Post-discussion Skills:

i.   Concluding notes of the discussion to be prepared carefully and noted down for future use.
ii. Compare them with earlier observations and resolve differences in an amiable manner if any.
iii. Implement the mutually reached appraisal plan so that the developmental works could be speeded up.
iv. Analytical review of appraisal procedures to keep them up to date.

On the basis of the above, we can conclude that the process beginning from pre-discussion to post-discussion stage points to only one thing and that is to maintain cordial atmosphere throughout. Our view is that the discussion procedure is more difficult than actual appraisal. If the appraiser succeeds in the former, he wins the hearts of all. Therefore, the appraiser ought to be very careful to establish and maintain cordial atmosphere throughout. It will minimize differences and make the appraisal procedures successful.

□□□□

CHAPTER 8

Bottlenecks in Teachers' Performance Appraisal

It is quite normal that industrial development and increase in production are two important areas in which all the organisations and corporate houses are deeply interested. But this is not possible without the workers' dedication to and attachment with their organisation. What the workers can do or not do directly effects the productivity of the organisation. That is why "appraisal" in industrial/commercial sector has assumed the greatest significance and is like a mutual contract between the employers and employees. In fact the appraisal system is a significant activity in the industrial sector. The appraisal pro forma prepared with mutual discussion and consent of the appraisers and appraisees play an important role in keeping the good health of the organisation as these exercises are based on democratic values. The whole system being democratic rarely dissatisfies anyone. On the other hand, it creates an atmosphere conducive to growth and development of not only the individual but the organisation also. Objective appraisal and mutual analysis of the appraisal results very easily boost up the appraisees' desire to improve her/his performance.

In fact in several of select areas like medical, chartered accountancy, law, architecture etc. in which registration is pre-requisite to enter the profession to practise it, performance appraisal in their respective areas is a significant criteria to be successful. Those not performing up to the mark can be moved against. Medical Council can take action against a practising doctor and Bar Council against a non-performing advocate. But in educational sector, there is no such authority which could fix standards and take action against a non-performer. There are several reasons for this:

8.1   Obstacles in Effective Appraisal in Education:

(i)   Inexperienced Managers in Education:

At school level the teachers' performance appraisal is normally made annually which is called annual confidential report. It is limited to government institutions. It is more customary and lacks objectivity. Subjectivity often creeps in. The appraiser (often the Head of the school) gives good report to those who he likes and average to the others. The department of education does inspection after two or three years. There is no such provision in colleges. There the teachers are performers as well as self-appraisers if their conscience pricks them to do which is very rare. The job is so secure that the education authorities feel helpless in taking action against a non-performer. Teachers' organisations are too strong and the education department looks like a pigmy before them. That is why performance appraisal is a herculean task in these institutions. On the other hand, responsibility of appraising the teachers in private institutions lies solely on the managers or the Heads. Except the Head, the managements consist of traders/businessmen who are adept in assessing profits and losses but are poorly equipped to appraise the teachers and the teaching schemes. They know very well how to raise ninety nine to hundred but know nothing about good education. Most of the management office-bearers or the members are not more than graduates who might not even heard the word "appraisal." In such situations, there remains only the Head of the institution who can perform the appraisal work to some extent. But the question arises how much the appraisal conducted by him is relied upon by the management and how many of his suggestions or recommendations are accepted by the authorities and how quickly they are acted upon. What is quite often seen that the recommendations of the Head after appraisals are dumped under the carpet due to reasons best known only to the managers which are mostly extraneous? Thus this exercise too is made redundant. Moreover, these types of hurdles could be overcome by strong will-power in the larger interests of the institution by taking the following steps: —

(a) At least the manager of the institution should be an educationist who is well aware of the aims of education and the methodologies to achieve them; is able to appraise not only the teachers' performance but also the available necessary infrastructure.

(b) In case any educationist is not available in the management for the post of Manager, such responsibilities should be given to the Head of the institution. In such situations, this is the best option.

(c) Since the Head is the executive officer of the institution, he remains is direct touch with the students, teachers and the parents; and knows very well the entire institution in its totality. So the management should never overlook his suggestions or recommendations.

(d) Sometimes, the management may get the appraisal work done by outside experts. It will help them compare the appraisal results by the Head of the institution with that of outsiders. It will also increase the trust of the teaching faculty in the Head and the management.

(ii)   Obscurity of the Educational Effects:

The by-product in education sector cannot be identified, explained and defined as in industries and other corporate. There is also no consensus on what are the aims and objectives of imparting education? Educationists differ drastically in this area. Is the aim of education to impart new knowledge to the child or to imbibe it in such a manner that he is able to use the acquired knowledge in his life later or to shape the personality of the child in a socially acceptable and useful manner or to develop life skills and values in him? These are the hottest point of discussion among educationists. Again, whether education is creative or developing self-dependence or developing commitment to cultural traditions etc. or to develop a scientific temperament so as to investigate every concept before accepting it often disturb the educationists?

Suppose due to reasons beyond control a person standing on his feet becomes dependent on others in future, will he be termed uneducated and the teacher as bad performer? The truth is that all these ideas are closely related to education. A student who has learnt very well how to be self-dependent, may in future be dependent on others due to any reason like being crippled in an accident? A student may be introvert today but may be so extrovert in future that he achieves unexpectedly. A student may be disciplined today but may be a law-breaker in future or vice versa. These are such possibilities which quite often occur.

The effect of teaching on each student will be different due to his family, social and psychological background. And then how can we measure ever changing mind or temperament of the human-beings in spite of good education? What we want to say is that though increasing knowledge and refining behaviour are the aims of education but how to measure (appraise) them is the biggest issue. That is why appraisal in education is a herculean task. Performance appraisal in those areas is easier wherein defining objectives is easy and production can be quantified like in industry or a sales outlet. But in education the product: increase in knowledge, creativity, refined behaviour or good manners cannot be precisely defined or measured. How then performance of teachers could be appraised precisely? Until the objectives are clear and well-defined, how the products could be measured?

Education means increase in knowledge, change in behaviour and be well-mannered. Teachers perform these tasks very well but these are not easily visible to the eyes like those products in industries in terms of numbers, quality and outer looks. Second, the refinement in behaviour is not a one day process. It is continuous and perennial which goes on proverbially "from the womb to tomb." It is a life-long process. And to appraise this process, we have to depend upon the feedback from various sources which is very often not easily possible due to their unavailability. That is why it is almost difficult to have a tailor-made policy or procedure for performance appraisal in the education sector. It could be easily understood from the fast changes that take place in an infant. His pronunciation, recognising his mother, father and other close relatives, learning to honour them and actually showing respect to them, learning to walk, falling down in the process and then getting up to retry and to be an expert later in these skills is a long process that starts from birth and goes on indefinitely. Another thing in this respect is more important. Every individual is different in his learning capacity. Some are fast learners whereas others are either slow or too slow. Others are average. The learning environment is the same for all and the teacher pays attention to all equally but they learn differently due to their learning capacity. How can we blame the teacher or the environment for slow learning of any student when others are found to be benefitting well from the same teacher and the environment? The teaching-effects are always intrinsic, hence neither visible to the eye nor measurable in terms of quantity and quality. Even if we try somehow to measure them, how can we ensure that the students are not responding artfully to please the teacher? In order to please or influence the teacher they may respond in the way they are actually not. Some students are carefree. They may be actually what the teacher expects them to be but for fun sake, they may not respond as the teacher expects them to. How performance appraisals of the teacher could be successful in such a scenario.

(iii) Lack of Consensus about Educational Philosophy:

The uncertainty about the aims in education sector brings the educationists at crossroads. Some emphasize providing free atmosphere to the students conducive to natural growth whereas others say the students need constant care and guidance in their development and leaving them unattended is not free from risks. Shanti Niketan (Today's Vishwa Bharti) founded by Rabinder Nath Tagore and Krishnamurti Foundation Schools founded by Jiddu Krishnamurti are very good examples to cite in this context. Both icons founded these institutions with their own unique educational philosophy. Besides these two, there are other institutions like DAVs and Sanatan Dharm institutions. Minority institutions like SGPC schools, Madarsas, Christian and Buddhist schools etc. too are there. The aims and objectives of these schools being religious are different from those of other institutions which are by and large secular. In minority institutions, students from their own community are given preference not only in admissions but also in distribution of other freebies. Various education commissions too tried to define the educational objectives but there is a remarkable variance in their recommendations. Not only this, even in country to country, state to state or institution to institution we find difference in goals. In such a scenario, the impact that the teacher leaves on his students on account of his behaviour and teaching work and the students' acceptability of the teacher is considered to be the aim of education which is obviously half-truth. For example, what impact of the personality of a particular teacher has on his students remains hidden and never appraised.

(iv) Invisibility of the Educational Results:

As said in the concluding part of the above paragraph, the impact of the teacher's personality and his moral teachings remains hidden and these cannot be immediately seen and appraised. The fact is that the effects of teaching in the beginning are invisible and they take years to get visible exposure. And by then the students might have left the institution and entered the second phase of their life which is actually the aim of education; making it just impossible for anyone to appraise his learning at the institution and the performance of the teacher. How much successful or unsuccessful they are in their life and how perfectly they are coping with social and family responsibilities never come to the notice of the appraisers. The teachers very well perform these duties to make their students fittest members of the society but the results of their performance are not immediately known to them. These long-term goals that the teachers achieve but remain unexposed are never tested. What is appraised is the effect of their academic teaching on the students.

(v) Dispute over the Role of the Teacher:

As the aims and objectives of education are disputed by the educationists, similarly the teachers' role too is not clear. Some say they should perform as "mentors" whereas others opine that they are just "fellow-travellers." Some say they are "knowledge-providers" whereas others claim them to be "facilitators." Some go to the extent of calling them "baby-sitters" which is highly ludicrous. The truth is that the teachers are all rolled into one: They are not only knowledge-providers but also facilitators, fellow-travellers and mentors too when the students go wrong. But these roles have never been defined and demarcated: That is where the limits of a facilitator end and those of mentor start. In such a situation, the appraisal too becomes difficult. In this context, the Indian philosophy seems to be more relevant and appropriate wherein the teachers have been compared to a potter and the pupils to pots that they are making. Saint Kabir's couplet is an example of it. He says that the teacher is like a potter and the pupil is like a pot. The Teacher gives mild blows to the pot with one hand from outside but simultaneously gives support by the other hand from inside to give it the proper and desired shape. Another saint places the teacher even above God and says if the pupil meets both together, he ought to pay obeisance to the teacher first.

Some people, keeping the present scenario in mind, may find a few observations in the above paragraph out of place. They may be right to some extent. But in the Indian society, even today the parents hand over their wards to the teachers and feel assured that they children are in safer hands. But in such a confusing scenario, it is very difficult to appraise the performance of the teachers.

(vi) Scarcity of the Standardised Appraisal Tools:

Another important reason due to which teachers' performance appraisal becomes difficult is the scarcity of standardized tools of teaching appraisal. Due to factor mentioned above, no standardized tools and procedures for accurate performance appraisal of teachers could be devised in the education sector which could be nationally used. Some efforts at institutional level have been made but due to diversity in aims and objectives; and teachers' role, these too remained confined to the institution concerned. But their usability and utility for appraisal have been questioned from time to time not only by the teachers but educationists too.

(vii) Teachers' Opposition to Appraisal:

The teachers too have been opposing the very idea and procedures in practice for their performance appraisal. They fear that its results will be used against their interests. Their increments will be stopped promotions denied and perhaps may even be demoted. So far promotions and annual increments have been given automatically and performance appraisal has been ignored. But now when performance appraisal is tried to be implemented, it creates suspicions in minds of the teachers which is not unfounded to some extent. And multiplicity of appraisers (managers, principals, parents, students etc.) is enough to send shivers down their spines. Still in some universities like Delhi, some thought has now been given to the teachers' performance appraisal; a code of conduct for teachers has been framed and implemented. Its results are still awaited.

8.2　Some Developments Influencing Performance Appraisal of Teachers:

As said earlier that some awareness about teachers' performance appraisal has increased. Some institutions have started inspiring their teachers for making self-appraisal. The departments of education too have realised their responsibilities in this context. They have started making teachers accountable to their duties. This has caused a ray of hope in the education sector too. Post-independence steps taken in this direction are following and their impact quite visible these days:—

(i)　Responsibility of Teachers Fixed:

There is no doubt that teachers' accountability has increased a lot in recent times and they are held responsible for any dereliction of their duties in any respect particularly with reference to their role towards their students. Reasons behind it are national as well as local. On national level, the recommendations of the several Education Commissions have brought fast changes in the then scenario. These commissions have tried to identify the educational aims and objectives, tried to define them and also have clearly emphasized the roles of the teachers in their realization. It has made the teachers more accountable to the achievement of these goals. Consequently, the society in general and the nation in particular have become more aware about the teachers' duties and their roles in the society's making and have started doing performance appraisal of the teachers on the basis of their wards' progress in informal manner. Unfortunately, the work of these commissions has been more or less investigative and recommendatory and the governments have pushed these reports under the carpet due to their political interests or pleading insufficiency of funds.

(ii)   Recent Developments Affecting Education:

Falling standards of education have had a ripple effect on the education departments and to control it they started taking revolutionary steps and their effects too are very well visible. Delhi government, alarmed by the falling standards of education in its schools had started making teachers accountable for this degeneration about five-six years back. The Parents-Teachers Associations were given some administrative responsibilities/powers like monitoring teachers' late coming, bunking classes, ignoring teaching, their way of teaching etc. The Central Board of Education, New Delhi too took some academic measures, developed educational tools, introduced new ways of students' evaluation called Continuous Comprehensive Evaluation scheme, trained the teachers in its use and instead of giving marks to the students, awarding grades has been introduced. Very good results of both have come to the fore and the results have very well improved. Similarly the well-established organisations like DAV have developed their text-books, devised new ways of students' evaluation and retrained their teachers on the basis of these text-books and the new methods of assessing students' progress by holding on-job-training programmes. Encouraging results of these changes have been pouring in so far. Sooner or later these schemes will be appraised and their usability or otherwise will be confirmed. It is good that the Central Board of Education, New Delhi has started involving parents in these schemes as well and has trained them in their monitoring so that these could be successfully implemented. Parents have also shown great interest in these changes. The teachers' performance appraisal too, may be informal will be made by the parents.

(iii)   Introspection on Educational Goals:

The foregoing discussion makes it one thing clear that due to fast social, economic, industrial and information technological changes taking place of late, there is a growing new interest on the educational aims and objectives which may fulfill current needs. The educational theories propounded by the educationists like Piaget, Bloom, Mager have drawn the attention of the educational policy makers and administrators because these theories focus on all the three aspects:

Cognitive, Affective and Psychomotor and repeatedly emphasise their classification, assimilation, accommodation and equilibration etc. This emphasis is not just limited to teaching. It is now being introduced to Teaching-Performance-Appraisal also so that the teachers could be made more accountable. The impact of this shift in thinking has started giving good and encouraging results which though are limited so far. By the development of new instructional goals, instructional strategies, instructional procedures and educational and evaluation tools etc. which could establish how far the educational aims and objectives could be achieved, it seems some positive changes are taking place in the education sector as well which is a good sign. Some more time it may take, but progress in this direction is now certain and performance appraisal of the teachers will be easier and more meaningful in the times to come.

(iv)   Use of New Techniques and Procedures:

These days new techniques of teaching are being used in some progressive institutions. These are staff differentiation, team-teaching, micro-teaching, individualized instruction, prescriptive teaching etc. This new approach has developed new thinking in education, has infused new energy among the teachers and has developed new interest in the teaching methods. Whereas in team-teaching, two or three teachers teach any complex topic together, in staff-differentiation experts in different fields join together to teach. Whereas in micro-teaching any complex topic is taught breaking it into smaller units and may be sometimes in smaller groups, in individualized teaching complex topics are explained to two to three students so that they understand the concepts well and assimilate them. Through these techniques all the available teaching manpower is utilized to the maximum in the best manner for the sake of the students who are seen to be benefitting very well by these new strategies. Teaching aims and objectives are well achieved and simultaneously very evaluated as well.

A few scholars while analyzing these techniques and procedures have criticized them. They find Staff differentiation as a threat and source of exploitation to their professional existence. Others consider micro-teaching as wastage of time and energy. They say how the teaching skills could be segregated. They are right to some extent. But it has to be judged and decided by the teacher-educators/ teachers when, how and for which concepts micro-teaching has to be used for making them more clear. And when staff differentiation is successful in engineering, medical, law etc., why it can be not useful in teaching? Moreover criticism and counter-criticism is part of each innovation. Therefore, the change makers need not worry about it and ought to continue with their reformatory process in the education sector. Yes, one thing is most important for success. The teachers, the real implementers of any scheme must be fully taken into confidence otherwise even good schemes are bound to crash to the ground without their support. This is very necessary as the new teaching schemes could be used only by the teachers who are well aware of them, have faith in them and are willing to implement them.

(v)   Information Technology: A Gift to Education:

Today information technology has brought revolutionary changes in the education sector also. The students get knowledge-enriched very fast using Google these days. They are today more aware of their teachers' roles and responsibilities and have started looking up to them for updating their knowledge regularly. They do not hesitate to use information technology to put their questions to their teachers in case of any doubt. Their general awareness has considerably increased. The teachers too are very well aware of their students' growing interests and their general awareness. So they reach their classes fully prepared to meet the new challenges. Though it has nothing directly to do with the teachers' performance appraisal but it is also true of the teachers that the better they answer their students' queries the better performers they will be. So they have also started updating their knowledge using Google. Though the information technology is available only in urban areas, still a good change has taken place which will soon reach rural belts also. Use IT has been found to be useful in man-management also. Researchers from Old Dominion University Virginia that Facebook profiles can be just as — if not more — accurate job performance indicators as self-reported personality tests. "You can also access a record of that person's past behaviour on their social media profile," said Katelyn Cavanaugh.

What preparations to be made before commencing upon for a successful teachers' performance appraisal and what expectations this exercise ought to meet, has been discussed in detail in the First Chapter and these ought to be kept ready for it.

8.3   Performance Appraisal Systems:

Keeping in mind all the factors discussed herein this book and before we start with planning the performance appraisal systems; we ought to decide who will be the appraiser and whether she/he is capable of performing this important job. Who will join this exercise to complete it in its totality? In other words, we know very well the stake-holders in education and their right i.e. the students and their parents. They ought to be involved in it. But it should be very well settled how much weight has to be given to the feedback from the students and their parents. As already discussed in detail in Chapter One, we had emphasized that the success of performance appraisal fully lies on the abilities and competencies of the appraisers. Therefore there should be no doubts about the appraisers while planning for the performance appraisal of the teachers.

Besides the above, other factors to be kept in mind while planning performance appraisal are: —

(i)   Facts Based Appraisal:

The appraisal should be made on the basis of areas provided by the teacher or the institution. The limitations of appraisal should be incorporated in the appraisal scheme in such a manner that these are not overlooked at any stage. It will help the appraiser to be as objective as possible.

(ii)   Immediate Feedback:

Feedback ought to be provided to the appraisee as soon as the appraisal concludes otherwise the exercise will be futile. Feedback should be given in writing and in clear terms.

(iii)   Accountability:

As we talk of accountability, it is not confined to the appraisee only. It includes Head of Department and the Management also. Since the HOD too comes into the ambit of performance appraisal in terms of whether his pre-determined aims and objectives were achieved or not, should he be a part of the appraisal team? Will his day to day appraisal of the appraisee in question be sufficient? And if he is included in the appraisal scheme, could he be as objective as he ought to be due to his possible likes and dislikes of the appraisee on account of his daily contacts with him? These are the issues which ought to be earnestly resolved before commencing upon the real exercise.

❑❑❑❑

CHAPTER 9

Human Resource Development, Appraisals and Rewards

What miracles a good appraiser/leader could do while developing human resources and how he could infuse new energy in them, has already been discussed in detail in Chapter Three. Now a question arises what after all is this Human Resource Development? It ought to be defined precisely to eliminate any doubts about this important topic. The performance appraisal cycle is closely attached with the personnel development. Without understanding the performance appraisal cycle, it is difficult to understand the human resource development. The tools used in the performance appraisal cycle too are too typical to be understood. Thereafter another question arises: What after all the performance appraisal cycle has to do with human resource development and how it helps the personnel in their professional development? If we look at it minutely we clearly notice that performance appraisal cycle, appraisal tools, human resource development and the stimulants go hand in hand. They are complementary to each other. None of them can exist alone. If one is detached from the other, the whole process becomes useless.

9.1   Development of Personnel:

The fact is that Human Resource Development starts covertly just from the moment the personnel enters the organisation for an interview on which an overt shape is given after her/his selection. What is expected of the personnel and what skills and expertise he possesses is appraised well before her/his selection. This developmental-process goes on till she/he leaves the organisation which is as important for the organisation as for the personnel under reference. The main steps of Human Resource Development are the following: —

(i)   Screening:

This is the procedure by which the managers choose the best personnel from the list of possible candidates keeping the present and future needs of the organisation. This procedure is completed using various techniques. One of them is viva voce. By this technique the managers try to judge the suitability of the candidate through face to face interaction. The interviews too are of various types. First is "Structured Interview" in which identical questions are asked so as to accurately compare one with the others. Second is "Unstructured Interview" by which the managers ask profession related and general questions keeping the organisation's goals in his mind and also to judge the analytical prowess of the personnel. Third "Probing Interview" by which the interviewer tries to probe into the professional history of the personnel to know his antecedents including his educational and professional qualifications, previous experience, special skills, dynamism and character in detail so as to judge his suitability to the organisation? This method is time consuming and costly. But keeping its advantages in mind, it is not a bad idea even if it is a bit costly and time consuming. Some organisations prefer Screening Written Tests too before face to face interviews to judge their general knowledge, professional and analytical skills.

Precautions during Interviews:

a.   At the time of interview, the atmosphere should be cordial, friendly and stress free. Seating arrangement must be comfortable. It will go a long way in making the glory of the organisation.

b.   Sometimes, the interviewers start indulging in leg-pulling trying to disparage the candidate and emulating themselves. It is not a good thing. The organisation will have to suffer from it. Hence this attitude ought to be discarded out rightly. It inhuman also.

c.   Sometimes, the atmosphere in the interviewing room becomes very humorous and therefore joyful. There is no harm in it. But the interviewers ought to keep the limits in their mind.

d. No questions ought to be asked which have no concern with the interviewee's profession or position for which he is being interviewed.

(ii)   Selection:

After interviews comes the process of selection of the most appropriate candidate on the basis of his records presented to the organisation. As far as possible the interview results should be declared just after the process is over so that the candidates are not left guessing and waiting. It is more important for the left out candidates also for the reason that they may be trying elsewhere also and for the selected too lest they opt out to join elsewhere due to the long wait. The interviewers must keep it in mind that talented employees do not wait for long. Even if the results are not declared just after the interview, the selected one should be called in confidence and told about his selection and when to join.

(iii)   Orientation:

The exercise of introducing the newly appointed candidates to the old employees of the organisation, its policies and work-culture is called orientation. During this exercise, the background of the organisation, its hierarchical structure, personnel policies, services and facilities provided by the organisation, its goals and other rules and regulations are brought to the notice of the newly appointed personnel so that they can assimilate themselves with the new organisation and work jointly with the old employees. It is also pointed out to them what the organisation expects from them for the achievement of their organisational goals. In the large organisations, these pieces of information are given to the new entrants in book form whereas in smaller ones, it is done orally. Workshops are held if there are any questions or doubts. Orientation is very necessary due to its advantages. This exercise brings a sense of job-security among the new entrants. They feel more carefree; feel satisfied after the organisation's efforts to enable them adjust to the new environment. A mutual understanding develops between the new entrants and the organisation. Needless to say that such an atmosphere will be more productive and ultimately beneficial for both.

(iv)   Training:

After orientation comes in-service training so that new entrants could feel at ease while working on their tasks. It further assists them to adjust to the new work-culture. Though such training is given keeping the objectives of the organisation in mind, still it will be more appropriate if its objectives are set beforehand lest the training goes off the rails. Pre-determined objectives (goals) are like lighthouses which show the right way to the trainers. Other objectives of such training sessions are: Preparing the employees to perform well as per organisational goals and be ready for performance appraisal, the procedure of which is also introduced to them. Training techniques that could be used keeping the goals in mind are: —

(v)   Training Systems:

(a)   Apprentice Training:

It is imparted to those who are new to the trade/job: For example, an apprentice training to a doctor, engineer, business graduate etc. under an experienced expert of the related field sent after the completion of the course. This way the new entrant in the field gets on job training and is equipped to deal with the cases independently. After teachers' training the teacher-trainees are also sent for teaching practice in a school where experienced teachers supervise his teaching, points out the shortcomings in his performance and advise how to rectify and improve. This type of training may be on-job as well as off-job. The examples given herein are off-job training.

(b)   On-Job Training:

This training is given to those who are newly recruited in any organisation. Its purpose is twofold: One orientation of the new entrant to the organisation. Second is to give some additional/latest know how to him. It is imparted generally under the supervision of any experienced senior. The new entrant is introduced with the work-culture of the organisation and he is clearly told about the organisational objectives and what the organisation expects of him for their achievement. It increases the confidence level of the new entrant.

Another advantage of this training is that it eliminates trial and error; and uselessness of any effort.

(c)   Off-Job-Training:

It is imparted when theoretical knowledge is being given or when face to face contact is to be established with the new entrants to the profession in order to provide skilled leadership and to stimulate them to perform better. The skilled experts impart this type of training through workshops and seminars quite often using lecture method.

(d)   Vestibule Training:

It is given to those trainees who have no practical knowledge of working on the job. The trainees are sent to the workshop or laboratories and directly observe experts working on the projects. First they observe; and when they are confident, they are actually put on the work so that he could master the skills of the job but strictly under the close supervision of the expert. This is often followed in the teaching sector also. When a teacher-trainee sees an expert teacher using different teaching skills himself in the classroom, he too learns them to use effectively.

9.2   Senior Subordinates' Appraisal:

Successful performance appraisal of each employee is a challenge for the managers. This has become more challenging when they face highly experienced subordinates. Such senior subordinates sometimes become egoists and a cause for concern for the Managements who are not in position to get rid of them in legal ways and still have to deal with them. Sometimes, they are found to be more competent even than the managers and appraisers. Most seniors have failed so far to cope with this new phenomenon because taking work from more experienced and skilled ones and then objectively appraise them is not a child's game. To be successful in such situation, the managers and the appraisers will have to be more adapting to these fast developing new trends. Our suggestion is that the managements should handle such situations using untraditional ways like giving them leading roles. On one hand it will solve their problem of dealing with more experienced and skilled personnel, on the other it will boost the morale of the personnel and they will start making more sincere efforts for the organisation.

Performance appraisal and motivation are complementary to each other. Encouraging good performance or improving average performance and getting rid of the dead wood among the work-force are part and parcel of this appraisal process. Encouragement may be in any form. Well designed and strategically planned performance appraisal is the backbone of any organisation. That is why the managers ought to devote their maximum time, effort and resources to develop the appraisal system. In order to understand the well designed and strategically planned performance appraisal system, we will have to pay our maximum attention to the following: —

(i)   Thorough Study of the Performance Appraisal Procedure.
(ii) Thorough knowledge of the Performance Appraisal Tools.
(iii) Thorough knowledge of features of the appraisal systems.
(iv) Competence in identifying problems and remedies to them.
(v)   Thorough understanding of which appraisal system will suit to cure any problem.
(vi) Fully understand the importance of feedback and quick action to provide it.

There are other issues also which ought to be paid attention to but, if the above are ensured, others automatically resolved. Therefore they need no special mention here. Now let us move to understand the performance appraisal procedure.

9.3   Procedure of Performance Appraisal:

Performance appraisal procedure has already been discussed in detail in Chapter Two. Here it will be sufficient to say and remind the readers that this procedure involves five major steps namely Performance Models, Employee's Performance, Comparison between the former and latter, Analysis of Personnel's Performance and Immediate Feedback. These are not only self-explanatory but also have been discussed in detail earlier; therefore these need no elaboration.

(a)   Performance Appraisal Tools:

There are several tools used for performance appraisal. Graphic Rating Scale, Management by Objectives, Paired Comparison Tool, 360 degree Evaluation Reviews, Computerized Rating Scales, Essay, Critical Incidents, Work Standards, Ranking, Forced Distribution, Forced Choice, Weighted Checklist Performance Reports, Behaviourally Anchored, Social Media is some of the tools which are used for performance appraisal. Most important is the selection of the most appropriate tool which could very well fit in the appraisal procedure and meet the demands as per requirements.

Graphic Rating Scale:

The Graphic Rating Scale has been widely criticised saying that it gives too much freedom to the appraisers. But the truth is that there is no shortcoming in the scale. If there are any discrepancies, those are due to its wrong use by untrained people or due to subjective attitude of the appraisers or drifting away from the appraisal areas. There is no basis for its uncalled for criticism. If it is used properly, it could be termed as the most reliable. Another objection of the critics of Graphic Rating Scale is that it cannot appraise immeasurable performances like honesty, sincerity, commitment etc. It is true. These qualities may not be directly connected to the performance of any employee, but there is no doubt that such qualities indirectly have a great impact on the performance of an employee.

Since these could be easily drawn and used, these are most popular among the appraisers. The factors on which the personnel are to be appraised are put perpendicularly on left hand and a 7 point scale is put horizontally of the scale. Each factor is valued on the basis of performance and noted down in the scale. At the end values of each factor are added. Please see Table No.3 below.

Table 3
Graphic Rating Scale

Name of the Teacher:						Date:	
Department:						Rating:	
Rating--------- ---------Factor	1 Unsatis- factory	2 Satisfac- tory	3 Fair	4 Good	5 Better	6 Best	7 Exem- plary
Quantity And Output							
Quality Accuracy, Clarity & Thoroughness							
Supervision Direction, Correction & Advice etc							
Punctuality Regularity, Promptness & Overall Dependability							
Accessibility, Audibility, Intelligibility & Legibility							
Total:							

(b)   Management by Objectives : MBO:

Second important tool is Management by Objectives. It is used for personnel of each level of the organisation. It is so popular that everyone gives priority to it because it is simple, most appropriate and easy to understand. According to this the seniors sit with their juniors and earmark goals, fix duties and accountabilities. These goals not only serve the purpose of performing well in the chosen direction but also as lighthouses for performance appraisal latter.

Management by Objectives has six steps. First of all the Head of the institution/organisation sets the goals of his institution which ought to be achieved before the next round of performance appraisal. Second step is to fix the responsibilities and accountabilities of the employees/teachers and tell in clear terms what the institution expects from them. The third step is to help/guide the teachers to set their own half-yearly or yearly objectives which they wish to fulfill before the appraisal and both the sets of objectives of the Head and the personnel ought to be compared, differences if any sorted out mutually to avoid any kind of conflict later on. As fourth step, copies of mutually set objectives should be prepared and given to the teachers/personnel that may help/guide them at each stage. Fifth step is to analyse the progress from time to time and the goals be revised or modified if need be. Sixth, the entire exercise ought to be studied, analysed and concluded in its totality. After this the procedure restarts. One important point here to which attention ought to be drawn is that the whole exercise is to be done with mutual consent of the teachers/personnel to win their confidence without which the goals could never be achieved.

Why this tool is most popular among managers as well as employees/teachers could well be understood by studying the procedure once again. It being based on mutual consent is the most favoured. It involves the personnel at each stage of the procedure. So they like it. The managers like it because it helps them achieve their institutional/organisational goals. This procedure keeps the objectives in the centre of the process and never allows them to go out of sight. It also promotes the system of delegation of powers or decentralization of powers which helps the seniors and to give them more time to focus on other important matters. On the other hand, the managers indirectly train their subordinates in leadership skills and produce future organisational leaders. It increases the confidence levels of the subordinates. Cordiality, continuity and well planning in this procedure make it most favoured one.

c.   Paired Comparison Tool:

The difference between Graphic Rating Scale and Paired Comparison is only this that the former appraises one personnel at a time whereas the latter makes a comparison of performance between two. It introduces a healthy trend of competition. One tries to do better than the other. It also helps the managers to identify the better performer to encourage him do further better and the average performer to improve. The factors of the appraisal are or could be the same as that of Graphic Rating Scale.

d.   360 Degree Appraisal Tool:

As the name suggests this tool is used to appraise each other from top to bottom. Juniors to seniors: All join it. It is not only seniors appraising the juniors but vice versa also. Not only the seniors or juniors, even peers including all stakeholders appraise each other. The available infrastructure for better performance is also appraised on five point scale. Thus it is not only human-resource appraisal but infrastructural also. For the effective use of this tool the following points ought to be kept in mind:

> Principal or the manager meets the teachers and chooses appraiser for each other. To maintain uniformity in the appraisal system, an appraisal pro forma is given to each which is to be used while appraising each other.

> After the appraisal, the filled up pro forma are handed over to the Principal/Manager. The appraiser also rates the resources on six point scale used during appraisal. The ratings (5: Abundant 4: Sufficient 3: Just sufficient 2: Insufficient 1: Inferior 0: Not at all) are recorded in the pro forma. Please see Table number 4.

> The Principal/Manager tabulates the data and summarizes the appraisal results. The performance is rated on six point scale and ratings (5: Exemplary 4: Best 3: Better 2: Good 1: Satisfactory 0: Unsatisfactory) are recorded in the pro forma. Please see Table No.4.

> On the basis of this summary, the Principal/Manager sits with the teachers/employees to discuss it jointly and make an action-plan to sort out the problems if any and improve their professional knowledge and work-experience; and hone up their working skills and expertise.

> All the employees or the seniors are appraised on the basis of the well-designed action-plan and it becomes a part of their service-book.

> These action-plans help the employees/teachers to improve their leadership skills in their respective fields of work and keep guiding them and also to become the basis of further appraisal procedures.

Special features of this tool are reflected in the above points in as much as it involves everybody of the organisation in the process, appraise all irrespective of his position and status in totality, not only appraise available manpower but also all the facilities and infrastructure available to the employees/teachers which is necessary for performing the duties well. The available data is recorded in a register under two categories so that they are analysed from time to time, developmental activities in the organisation are taken up regularly and the personnel's work keeps improving.

Table 4
360 Degree Appraisal Matrix

Name of the Teacher: Date:						
Department: Rating						
Infrastructure Used—	5 Abundant	4 Sufficient	3 Just Sufficient	2 Insufficient	1 Inferior	0 Not At All
Teacher's Performance						
5 Exemplary						
4 Best						
3 Better						
2 Good						
1 Satisfactory						
0 Unsatisfactory						
Analysis:	Abundantly Skilled & Equipped	Sufficiently Skilled & Equipped	Just Skilled & Equipped	Insufficiently Skilled & Equipped	Poorly Skilled & Equipped	Miserably Unskilled & Equipped

Keeping this analysis in mind an action plan is prepared with mutual consent for further professional development of the manpower irrespective of his status or position in the organisation. The objectives of this plan are not only reformatory but also for professional development of the personnel, to provide them long-term service benefits and to reward them for excellent performance. All types of guidance like individual guidance, shifting to other duties keeping his progress in mind, providing leading roles, curriculum, workshops or further studies are provided to the personnel during this action-plan. After the making of action-plan full responsibility is given to the personnel so that he could implement the policies independently. The Principal/Manager is present with him but never interferes in his work until the personnel so desires for guidance. After the completion of the action-plan, the 360 Degree Evaluation restarts.

e.   Computerized Rating Scales:

Performance appraisal being a sensitive job cannot be left fully to machines but the computer technology has crept into appraisal domain too. Today such computer programmes are available which make the appraisers work easy. But it too has limitations because it works only according to the programme fed in it. It will remind the dates of the appraisal as programmed without keeping the unpreparedness (may be due to an illness) for appraisal of the employee in mind because it has "no mind" and insensitive to the employee's state of mind. And reminding an employee when he is mentally disturbed, will naturally be nagging to him. It is impossible for a machine to be sensitive to human sensibilities. So such a sensitive matter should not be left to machines only. These could be usefully used by the appraisers but very sensibly lest the very purpose is lost.

f.   Essay:

Essay is also used by the appraisers profusely in which they write the weak and strong points of an appraisee in an essay form and it is further used to prepare performance appraisal report latter. One major defect of this tool is that the appraiser focuses only on what is going on in present and ignores the working-history of the employee whereas appraisal always means an "appraisal in totality" which ought to keep the immediate past working of the employee in mind as well. Suppose a worker cannot perform in an expected manner due to any eventuality (like a sad happening in his family) but has been very good performer throughout, then injustice will certainly be done to him if only his present is considered. Secondly, essay is always by and large subjective. The appraiser focuses only on weaknesses of the appraisee. In case he notices any strong point of the appraisee, he notes it also down but unenthusiastically. Whether the appraiser wishes or not, an essay becomes an exercise in subjectivity leaving several aspects untouched. Third, it is always difficult to analyse an essay objectively. It depends fully on the appraiser whether he does justice or injustice with the appraisee. Fourth, the appraiser ought to have a perfect command on the language to be an essay writer. How many appraisers have this type of command?

a.   Critical Incidents Technique:

In critical incidents technique the appraiser notes down the plus and minus points of the appraisee incident by incident and prepares his notes. After the appraisal is over, he prepares his report based on these notes. The good feature of this tool is that it appraises a person in totality. This technique could also be best used only by those appraisers who have perfect command over their linguistic skills.

b.   Work standards:

While using this tool earlier established goals are kept in mind. When appraising an employee using this tool, it is tried to see whether the employee has performed according to already set standards of the organisation or not. These standards are set on the basis of time taken in production, its quality and quantity which serve as light-houses for the employees. That is why this tool is useful in manufacturing units only. This tool is unique because of its perfect objectivity. Its use in education could be limited.

c.   Ranking:

As the name suggests, the appraisers use ranking procedure while appraising any person and put him in the place/grade as he deserves according to his scored rank. It also facilitates the appraisal in its totality and the best performer gets rewarded and the worst further guidance how to improve.

d.   Paired Ranking:

Another form of Ranking Tool is Paired Ranking in which total appraisal of one employee is compared with the total appraisal of other one. But it has a few flaws. One, it disparages the low performers by de-motivating and demoralizing them when they are compared with better ones. Second, it seems as this technique does not rank the employees on the basis of objectives but on the basis of the performance thus ignoring and leaving the objectives aside or not giving much care to them. Thus the one who achieved the objectives a bit late gets neglected and remain unrewarded. It demoralizes the slow achievers.

e.   Forced Distribution:

Under this technique the appraiser makes groups of the appraisees and then assigns job to them. On the basis of their performance, he assigns the ranks in "ranges." This technique is significant in as much as it makes double appraisal: One individual and the other in groups. Second significance is that instead of categorizing the individual as best or otherwise, it ranks the group which promotes a sense of joint responsibility among the personnel. The team works to achieve their goals in collective spirit. But its one disadvantage is that it is unfit for individual appraisal because the rank is given to the group not to the individual.

f.   Forced Choice:

In forced choice the appraisal is made on the basis of a set of selected statements which more or less apply to each employee. One advantage of this tool is that the list of statements is uniform and the appraiser has no choice to move out. But it is a disadvantage also because other aspects of an employee's work remain un-appraised because of its limited statements on which it works. It also puts a question whether the employees get appraised by this technique appropriately or not.

g.   Weighted Checklist Performance Reports:

In Weighted Checklist Performance Report the appraiser fills up the same type of pro forma as used in Forced Choice performance form which too has a set of selected statements having different weights related to the employee's on-job and general behaviour. The appraiser does not know each question's/statement's weight. He responds to each question/statement either positively or negatively. The appraiser tries to be as objective as possible but being confined to a set of few statements, he has to stay within those limits irrespective of the fact whether the statements really brings out the reality about the employee or not. Such an appraisal may deterrent to the employee's professional development.

h.   Behaviourally Anchored Rating Scales:

This tool, short-named as BARS, uses Traditional Rating Scales and the Critical Incidents Technique simultaneously. The data related to employee's effective and ineffective behaviour is collected through Critical Incidents Technique and is analysed in an objective manner and then ranked on the scale being used by the appraiser. Since this tool covers a lot of job-behaviour, it is acceptable to a majority of the people in the organisation. With reference to a specific job, the behaviour of an employee is expressed in statement forms which vary between the most positive and the most negative. For example take Appraisal Skills. If any employee is appraised on the basis of appraisal skills and if he is found to be excellently equipped or badly equipped with these skills, then the appraiser will choose:

(i)   This person having a keen eye will be an excellent appraiser.
(ii) This person has fair grasp of appraisal skills and may be helpful to others.
(iii) This person if trained well may be a good appraiser.
(iv) This person having poor analytical acumen may be spared from appraisal work.

In order to rate the employee, such statements are prepared beforehand and are used accordingly. Instead of using adjectives like "Excellent" or "Worst" This tool is very effective for describing job-behaviour of an employee by explicit statements and leaving no ambiguity between the two extremes of Excellent and Worst. Critics of this tool say that it gives importance more to performance than production. But the objection seems to be ludicrous because if the performance is good, production too will be better.

i. Social Media Tools:

In recent times the managers/employers have started using social media like facebook, You-tube and twitter etc. to know more about their employees or the potential employees. It may not be directly related to the workers' performance even then it is a good source of knowing their minds: What they think about their superiors, their organisation and its working environment etc. which ultimately helps the employers/managers to appraise themselves and also to appraise their working or potential employees. And it is true to a great extent because on these social media sites, the user expresses himself freely which gives a lot of clear indications what is going on in his mind. The comments of the users on these social media about what projects the employees have done, what equipment like smart phone, Ipads, laptops etc. they are using, give a fair knowledge about them. The employers/managers have started to judge their employees' Tech-smart Quotient through these social sites. This step is not only commendable but also in tune with changing universal scenario in which Tech-smart employees only can deliver results. There are several instances when the people interacted online with like-minded people and found out unique solutions to any problem. Please refer to Chapter 10 in this connection.

9.4 Advantages of Performance Appraisal:

We have already discussed the importance and objectives of performance appraisal in detail in the First Chapter and its advantages cannot be different from them. Still there is no harm if these are reviewed once again. A majority of managers from corporate or education sector take performance appraisal as a technique to improve production in quality as well as quantity. Besides this, performance appraisal has other objectives also. And most of them achieve these objectives. But the problem arises when we start expecting good results just after one or two appraisals and after getting poor or unexpected results, stop doing it forgetting that it is a never ending process which ought to commence even from employee's entering the organisation and continue till the he leaves. Therefore the expected objectives of performance appraisal could be achieved only through goal oriented, well-designed and continuous comprehensive appraisal schemes. Productivity of the employees could be increased in quality and quantity only by sustained efforts which will be useful for Human Resource Planning as well as Manpower Management.

(i)   Human Resource Planning:

The best advantage of performance appraisal is to provide department-wise relevant information about manpower needs at each level of the organisation in terms of number and specialization. New recruitments are made on the basis of this feedback. Departmental promotions are also made keeping the performance of any person in mind. Need-based recruitments and performance-based promotions keep the internal system of the organisation in place. Performance appraisals also help the managers to be ready to fill up the gap in case any rank falls vacant due to any eventuality. Such preparedness could be assured only through continuous comprehensive performance appraisals only.

(a)   Recruitments and Selections:

The new recruitments guided by performance appraisal results function like light-houses for the man-power planners/managers on the basis of which they advertise, hold interviews and select the new employees and take further steps for their on-job-training, reorientation and smooth assimilation into the organisation.

(b)   Professional Planning and Development:

Professional planning and development can be made on the basis of the organisational or individual objectives. But our view is that both cannot be separated. Yes, we can make the organisation employee centric which will give the employees mental satisfaction due to a secure environment. They will be more committed to their organisation if it is employee centric and keeps their welfare always in its mind. Its benefits will ultimately and certainly reach the parent organisation. But it is also true that in order to give a desired direction to professional planning and development, the performance appraisal plays an important role in it by pinpointing the strengths and weaknesses of the employees so that the low-achievers could be timely guided to professionally develop or the excellent achievers could be timely motivated to do better in future. It will ensure professional development of the individual employee as well as the development of the organisation.

(c) Training and Development:

Keeping the above results and experiences in mind, we may conclude that a successful performance appraisal also provides need-based training of the employees on the basis of which the organisation plan further training programmes, hold workshops and sponsor the employees for studies/training outside the organisation. For example, if the teachers are found to be deficient in preparing lesson plans, really a tough job, during their performance appraisal, the institutions may hold training sessions/workshops to train the teachers in lesson planning. Similarly other areas found to be weak, could be strengthened through training sessions. A successful performance appraiser always tries to identify the weak and strong points of any employee's functioning and brief the organisation on the basis of his appraisal. Then the onus lies on the organisation to take necessary remedial steps for the benefit of the individual employee benefits of which will reach it automatically.

(d) Providing Incentives:

If good performance is not rewarded in time, it is likely to have negative effects not only on the employees but the organisation also. Motivation is very important. Timely special increments and promotions go a long way in organisational growth also. It increases the professional and self-esteem of the employee concerned. When an employee performs any special task successfully and if he is praised by the organisation, he feels highly elated and motivated to do better in future. Most of the organisations depend on performance appraisals for these motivating acts. And this is right too. As an employee performs, he gets the rewards in cash or kind, in the form of increments, promotions or cash awards in the same proportion. Therefore, the appraisal should be accurate: Lest a deserving employee is left out and undeserving gets the rewards.

(e) Identifying Incapable Employees:

There is another advantage of successful appraisal and that is to identify non-productive employees. There is no doubt that performance appraisers must help the low-achievers but there are occasions when all efforts made to improve the performance go waste and the employee becomes a liability for the organisation. Then what is the need to bear with such employees. But this job of getting rid of low-achievers is very sensitive. It needs to be handled with great care because a single wrong or hasty step may spoil the entire atmosphere of the organisation. Therefore, the trade union must be taken into confidence. First of all, appraisal procedures should be as transparent as possible and all should be fully aware of day to day happening in this area. Removals should not only be justified but seen to be justified also. Similarly demotions, layoffs, transfers and terminations etc. should also be fully justified. No hasty steps be taken in this respect.

9.5   Good Performance Rewards:

In the first chapter we have already acknowledged the rights of the managements who to reward or who to not. But rewards to good performers and high achievers must never be delayed otherwise it will have counter-effects. The deserving must be rewarded immediately. Old saying also goes that hit the iron when it is hot to give it a desired shape. If reciprocated immediately:

(1) It encourages the good performer.
(2) He feels elated.
(3) It initiates healthy competition among employees.
(4) Good performer when acknowledged serves as a role-model for other employees.
(5) Rewards could be extrinsic as well as intrinsic; but the former are more effective as they serve as morale-boosters.

Extrinsic rewards may be cash prizes, special pay-hike, special increments or in the form of special facilities or status. Extrinsic rewards are preferred by those who have more family responsibilities and want cash quite often; are very ambitious and want their diligence to be rewarded immediately and feels elated in saying that they are getting so much salary. Many rewards are extrinsic still they give inner peace to the employees as they feel proud of getting them.

Intrinsic rewards are appropriate for those employees who are self-satisfied, do not have many desires, are not much burdened by family needs and perform their duties as worship. But such employees could be counted on finger tips. Some employees like both types of rewards. But such employees are really rare who never expect rewards because they are so much satisfied with their work-performance that they do not need any motivation. Such employees are self-motivated. Oral back up, patting the back, praising work and conduct, motivating others publically to emulate a good performer, presenting with a commendation certificate, praising before a senior officer etc. are some of the forms of an intrinsic reward.

The managers, who are experienced and have far eyesight, sense the expectations of their employees immediately and oblige them with both types of rewards. Understanding the feelings of the work force may be a difficult task but it is not so for experienced and far sighted managers/employers.

❑❑❑❑

CHAPTER 10
Managements' Awakening

When the global scenario has been fast changing due to democratic values getting strengthened day by day, clinging to the past which causes hurdles in development looks to be entirely outdated. What to talk about these changes, even the terminology in managing industry has been fast changing of late. "Weaknesses" are called "developing fields", "employees/workers" are being termed as "colleagues", the "Supervisor/Boss" are being called "Line Managers", and "handicapped" are labelled with more humanely as "Differently-abled". What we want to emphasise is that the entire scenario from language to working styles has been moving ahead very fast. Juniors have been getting knowledge and experience from the seniors since ages but today, even the seniors at least in the industrial sector references of which were published in Times of India dated October 10, 2012, if they have the desired insights to do so, have been trying to enrich their knowledge and experience by observing their juniors reactions to a particular working situation and their handling. If the industrial sector has taken the initiative, why should the education sector lag behind?

Anjni Madhavi Kappagntula Senior Director Programme Management Operations Yodee India says:

"I would like to share an instance really taught me something that I cherish — the direct correlation between the art of practicing excellence and that of saying 'no'. Amol Borkar, my colleague was pretty methodical and would handle all the projects with extreme precision. He would have his fingertips on every minute detail of the areas he would handle and would ensure that all the points of failures were identified early in the life cycle to have a way of mitigating any risks that we may encounter. One thing I disliked about him was that during the allocation of assignments he used to say 'no' when he was given more work. He was not ready to take more; this irked me. But as I noticed that whatever he does, he strives for excellence and is not comfortable in taking more assignments and under-performing. He has mastered the art of excellence and clearly knows what he could do well and when to say 'no'. He has been a true inspiration for me and today, whenever I think of practicing excellence, I also tell myself that the desire to excel must be complemented with the ability to know when to say no."

Appreciating strengths of the employees and providing them facilities accordingly so that they could develop more in the right direction is also the foremost duty of the performance appraisers. Kavita Rao Director and Head of HR Unisys India emphasizes:

"I would like to talk about Asif Pasha, who joined Unisys as an office boy and later rose to the level of a system support analyst. Pasha came from an humble background and struggled hard to make both ends meet. We often noticed this shy unobtrusive young guy working quietly with his English dictionary or grappling with mathematical problems in a corner of the pantry. Spotting his talent, the organization gave him opportunities to grow and within a few years, through sheer hard work and dedication, Pasha became a system support analyst and has earned several awards and recognitions. For me, Pasha reinforces the fact that hard work and opportunities go hand in hand. The inspirational fact about Pasha is his tenacity, even in the face of challenging circumstances. He was never too proud and never let something be too difficult to try. His ability to leverage available opportunities, adaptability to every role that he took on and willingness to go that extra mile are great learning. I think the message is that had hard work and dedication pay, often sevenfold."

Learning and enriching one's knowledge with new insights by observing the juniors is not only indicative of one's large-heartedness but helps in opening new vistas to handle anticipated events a lot. Pankaj Arora Managing Director, Protiviti Consulting expresses his views in this connection in the following words:

"Sharing is a learning instance from a single employee would be difficult as I try to learn constantly from my people around.

Sometime back, when we were handling a manufacturing project, we had a junior consultant who did the project report for the client. In his report, he had mentioned about the use of a new technology which could help the client in energy efficiency. I was surprised to see that and asked him how he got to know about the technology. To my surprise, he said that he researched on the internet and talked to a few people about it and included it in the report. The client also appreciated the report. The consultant did not have any engineering background nor any work experience. I learned from him that if you have desire to learn and know things, your education or line of knowledge is no constraint for you. He taught me not to draw boundaries and limit yourself; the hunger and passion to learn new things could always take you to higher levels."

These three examples emphasise how the seniors learnt a lot by observing their juniors closely. They could perfectly identify their strengths. Not only they appreciated their juniors but also learnt a lot from them which they could not even when studying for their higher degrees or undergoing training sessions. These are the new facets of performance appraisal which all the appraisers ought to take cognizance of.

Under such changing times and attitudes, the education sector should also come forward and start the new process of self-learning from all resources that come their way. The performance appraisers will have to shed their orthodox views and dictatorial attitudes and replace them with which are more progressive, democratic, suitable to changing times and conducive to modern working styles.

Once I had had a chance to learn a lot from the plain-speaking of one of my students. It so happened that on prolonged listening of "bhutni ka" from my teacher-father, I developed the bad habit of calling an erring student "bhutni ka" (Son of a she-ghost). Most of the students had had a hearty laugh at it which often reduced their tensions too. Once when I labelled so an erring student he complained, "Sir, Wrong-doer I am and you are accusing my mother. Do you know how much intelligent she is?" I was awestruck. Then and there I resolved never to use that nomenclature for any one in future. My bad habit was thus uprooted on account of my plain-speaking student.

I recall another interesting incident. One teacher from Bihar used to pronounce (The sound of '*ksh*') as (*Chh*). Once he got angry on one student and ordered in Hindi to get out of the class. The boy replied, "Sir, If I go out of my *kachha* then you will run away from the *kaksha* (classroom). The students laughed hilariously. The readers must have got the cue of the humorous interpretation by the students. At this the teacher got more furious. He brought the whole laughing class before me. I counseled the students to behave properly in future and let them go, knowing well that they were also right in laughing at the teacher's commands. After the students left, when I drew the teacher's attention that in Hindi the men's underwear is called *kachha* he too laughed hilariously and modified his pronunciation for future. Thus the student taught his teacher the right pronunciation. Both these incidents made the teachers to learn their lessons which were overdue for long.

The fact is that performance appraisal is carried out by the managements but the question arises how much competent the managements are in doing accurate appraisals. More important question is how much eager they are to learn from those who they appraise. And the most important is the interaction of the managements with the appraiser on the appraisal report. It is often seen that most of such meetings are just customary. The appraiser and the managements meet have tea and toast, gossip about and disperse. The maximum they do is to discuss only cases of those employees whose performance is below expectations. Without giving much care to the reasons due to which the employee might have achieved low, they out rightly take disciplinary action and feel satisfied that they have done their right job. Under such circumstances the appraisee start feeling disheartened whereas the appraiser guilty of being a party to the wrong decision. Such situations cannot be called good either for the appraiser or employee or the organisation.

The managements and the appraisers ought to avoid such situations. We have said many a times before that appraisal is a continuous, never-ending process for professional and institutional development. Neither should it be overlooked or neglected or any crucial decisions taken in haste. The appraisal report must the thoroughly studied, analysed and reviewed with a humane manner. Then the employee should be given opportunity to what he wants to say about his performance. Then suggestions for improvement and more so due opportunity/time to carry out the suggestions should also be given to the employee. Stringent actions should be taken only as a last resort in unavoidable circumstances.

In such situations the Human Resource Department can play a vital role. If it wants to avoid any undesirable developments in its organisation then it needs to keep the continuity, regularity, punctuality and objectivity in performance appraisal processes. It will have to keep designing and redesigning appraisal plans, ensure their timely execution and implementation in a systematic manner. When designing the appraisal plans they should mutually draft appraisal policies, choose appropriate appraisal techniques, prepare appropriate formats for appraisal reports, take time-bound, relevant and logical decisions on the appraisal reports and ensure continuous interaction between the appraiser and appraisee so that both are clear about their roles and expectations from each other. The organisational objectives need to be thoroughly understood by the employee and it is the Human Resource Department that does this crucial job as it has to maintain a balance the employee's professional objectives and institutional ones. Only then the organisation will grow and the employees develop to their satisfaction.

An ideal performance appraisal is that which gives satisfaction to both: The appraisee and the appraiser. Both should feel contented what they did during the appraisal process. But the ease, with which this feature of appraisal is mentioned, is actually not so simple and easy to do an ideal and successful performance appraisal. The appraisee should not feel scared of this exercise. Rather he should take it as a part of his duty or responsibility to the organisation he is working in and he should gladly extend his full cooperation in carrying it out because it is the appraisal of his work which will present a true picture of the quality of his performance, provide him more opportunities to unfold his talents and skills and open new vistas for his individual and professional growth. It is the only trustworthy channel for the management to know about its work-force, its qualities, their profession and individual needs which help it not only to focus on the organisational objectives but also on the individual needs of the work-force so that they are fully satisfied and are able to render their best in return for their organisation. Thus performance appraisal is satisfying and gratifying for both: The work-force and the organisation. As a result of this type of productive environment, the managers are always ready to introduce new ideas and adopt new techniques in the running of their organisation.

10.1   Fixing of Goals and Performance Standards:

Though the performance appraisal of an employee starts from the very beginning when he comes to interact with the managers to be part of any organisation but it gets a formal shape when the employee and the organisation's policy makers and implementers meet to discuss ways and means to ensure better working of the organisation. The objectives of the organisation are spelled out before the employee and he is clearly told what the organisation expects from him. If the employee puts any problem or expresses any difficulty before the management, all efforts are made to sort them out. Essential equipment, tools, environment conducive to better working are provided and the back-up policies are explained to him so that he could work efficiently and with coordination with the organisation.

As said earlier that the organisation's objectives function as lighthouses for the employees as well as the organisation, especially when it initiates performance appraisal. These are objectives which decide the way how the employee has to proceed for better performance and its appraisal latter on. The objectives need to be standardized. Better if they are observable and measurable also. They should not be unrealistic. If the objectives pass the test of these qualities, these will certainly be very effective.

Performance standards are those pre-determined norms which were earlier established by the employees by their exceptional performance which show the present workforce a way to perform on the same standards or better than those. These norms also support the already defined expectations of the organisation explicitly for their employees. For example one objective of an educational institution could be: If a parent visits the institution, the teacher concerned must attend to him at the earliest and solve his problem within half an hour and if the teacher succeeds in doing so, it is an example of his good performance according to already settled norms. Another objective could be: The teacher will reach his class within 5 minutes of the shift over and if any teacher follows it and always reaches his class within 5 minutes, it will be an example of his good performance on the basis of punctuality. The standardized objectives should be defined in terms of quantity so that they could be accurately measured while being appraised.

10.2   Performance Appraisal: The Logic:

The foregoing paragraphs clearly indicate the importance of performance appraisal. It is the duty of the managers that they continue doing the appraisal regularly to ensure achievement of not only institutional/organisational goals but meeting individual professional objectives also. The appraisal ought to be based on healthy appraisal policies and procedures. If the institution/ organisation needs to keep its clientele happy and fully satisfied, then the appraisal should be fully in tune with the already set standards. Some educational institutions like DAVs in the country are very popular among masses because they keep the standards intact and they follow zero tolerance against any dereliction of the duties. The work and conduct of the employees/teachers is monitored and guided by these performance appraisals. The managers have a right to know how much better their employees/teachers have been doing and whether that is in tune with their expectations or not. The employees/teachers also have a right to know how their work is being appraised and whether it is being appreciated or not, what are they going to get for their good performance and how their performance is going to influence their professional life. It will be pertinent to point out here that the students and their parents are the consumers of educational institutions. Both should feel assured what they are being provided by the educational institutions is of good quality and for their betterment. Therefore the teachers and the education managers must see that both remain highly satisfied.

10.3   Managerial Roles in Performance Appraisal:

The management is accountable for regular, continuous and hurdle-free appraisal of its employees/teachers and for providing good educational facilities to the students. It should provide all those facilities, favourable environment, necessary tools and/or equipment which are essentially needed for better academic performance. Only those objectives ought to be appraised which were identified mutually. Those topics should never be included in the appraisal schemes which were not agreed upon. The appraisal areas should be limited so that it does not become unmanageable and is carried out successfully. The appraisees should be given this much liberty that they may make/take decisions independently according to times and circumstances. It will ensure not only their performance goes on without any interruption but also develop in them a sense of being important having abilities to take independent decisions. It will help in the development of leadership skills in the employees/teachers.

10.4   Teachers' Responsibilities:

The performance policies need to be thoroughly understood by the employees/teachers and religiously followed not only for their own good but for their institution as well. Duty is worship: Ought to be their motto. They should do all that which helps in the achievement of the institutional/organisational goals. Whereas the managements ought to be very clear about their objectives, the employees should know clearly how to achieve them and both should keep continuously interacting in this context. Any communication gap between the two will certainly be deterrent to individual growth and organisational development. The employees should also make it their habit to keep self-appraising themselves as this is the best kind of appraisal and must keep a close watch on those attitudes or habits which are counterproductive and hindrance to achievement of set goals. If they need to make any changes in their work strategy, they should immediately inform their seniors so that the latter are also fully familiar with the day-to-day functioning of the organisation. It will reduce any possible difficulty in the smooth running of the organisation.

Now the question arises whether the teachers and academic managers are performing well? Sorry to say that they have not been doing well in recent times otherwise there would not have been so much violence in the educational institutions all over the world. The students, especially the boys, are getting very aggressive these days. News items in dailies prove it. This is a clear indicator that the students' energies are not being channelized properly. It is an alarming situation. It needs to be taken care sooner the better.

10.5   Duties of Human Resource Department:

The importance of Human Resource Department in the performance appraisal process cannot be overlooked. The appraisal criteria are decided by it. Appraisal designs are drawn by it. The whole procedure is implemented by it. It keeps a close watch on the process. It analyses the appraisal results and maintains all the records. When any employee is to be appraised and who to do this exercise, notifying the person concerned about the dates, time and place: All are in Human Resource Development Department's domain. Not only this, it also provides feedback to the appraisers about the quality of appraisal carried out by them so that discrepancies if any could be removed lest they creep in further appraisals. It ensures immediate feedback to the appraisees; invites their objections if any and takes steps for their grievance-redressal. In case the performance of most of the employees of any department is found to be below expectations, the HR department makes arrangement for on-job-training or takes any other appropriate steps to overcome the general weakness in the employees' performance. It also reviews its recruitment policies and/ or On-Job-Training programmes in the light of poor performance of the employees.

10.6   Pre-appraisal Discussion:

As pointed out several times earlier also, interaction between the appraiser and appraisee is very necessary. It helps the appraiser to understand his role and responsibilities. The appraisee briefs him about the appraisal area and his objectives. It also helps both to understand the appraisal methodologies and procedures very clearly. Doubts if any are discussed before the actual exercise begins. The appraiser takes the appraisee in full confidence, ensures him that the exercise will fully be objective, unbiased and within the agreed limits; and is not to harm but to help him to do better in future. Both decide upon those steps which would help in successful appraisal and will build mutual confidence. The important points that the appraiser ought to keep in mind before the exercise begins or during the appraisal procedure or after that are given below: —

10.7 Duties of the Appraiser:

(i)   The appraiser ought to be fully aware of his duties and their importance if performed well. A minor mistake or carelessness on his part will send wrong signals to the appraisee.

(ii) The appraiser must define his and the appraisee's role in the performance appraisal before actually proceeding on it. The appraisee must be informed who, when and how will he appraise him.

(iii) The appraiser should also first analyse the expectations of the appraisee so that he could appreciate them well.

(iv) In order to know the background of the appraisee, the appraiser should apprise himself of his skills, training, work-experience and any special qualifications very well.

(v)   The appraiser ought to know the organisational, individual and professional objectives well; and must analyse them beforehand with reference to already set goals so that he remain focused while appraising the employees.

(vi) He should also have pre-discussions with the appraisee with reference to the work-expectations, appraisal areas, organisational objectives and pre-determined goals and develop a consensus in this regard.

(vii) He should explain the appraisal procedures and give other relevant information to the appraisee before starting with the actual exercise. The appraisee must be aware of all the facts about the appraisal techniques. He should not be kept in dark at all.

(viii) The appraiser should train the employees in self-appraisal also. The latter should be well aware of its importance.

(ix) After self-appraisal, its analyses are also necessary. If the appraisee brings any new facts to the notice of the appraiser, he must take its cognizance, include it in the appraisal scheme and tell the appraisee also about it.

(x)   The appraiser should review all relevant documents of the appraisee, take note of critical incidents, his work-standards, regularity and punctuality and very well analyse them.

(xi)   The appraiser needs to analyse the work-behaviour and the standards of his performance appraisal during the appraisal period. The more the appraisee keeps a balance between the two, the better his performance would be.

(xii)   The appraiser should prepare the final appraisal report after the procedure is over. What steps like rewarding, further training, cautionary notes, warnings etc. need to be taken for better growth and development of the appraisee and the organisation, for setting up new targets; and what follow-up-action to be taken in case of performance being below expectations must be clearly mentioned.

(xiii)   If any action not related to performance is noticed by the appraiser during appraisal procedure he must take its cognizance to discuss it with the appraisee and to provide guidance in this context.

(xiv)   What avenues of progress or hurdles in its way for the appraisee will open up after the performance appraisal need to be thoroughly discussed at the appropriate level like appraisees' senior officer or the Human Resource Department and the appraiser should fully geared up for it.

(xv)   The appraiser should be ready to handle disagreements or on promotional avenues after the appraisal with the appraisee and be equipped to remove them.

10.8   Precautions in Preparing the Appraisal-Plan:

(i)   Action plan should not be crowded with other areas. Appraisal should be confined to the area agreed upon with the appraisee so that the procedure remains manageable.

(ii)   Examples and references to clear any point should be crystal clear, accurate, unbiased and definite; and there should be no hesitation in reviewing them.

(iii)   The suggestions given for performance, reinforcing any desirable behaviour or to motivate the appraisee should be beyond any doubts. They should be clear, comprehensible and implementable.

(iv)   The environment should remain positive so as to find solutions to the problems if any arising during performance appraisal and to reduce chances of any controversies.

(v)   Enforcement and reinforcement need to be provided immediately wherever felt necessary.

(vi)   Developmental points must be identified and noted down during the performance appraisal so performance of the personnel gets a boost and further planning for appraisal on their basis could be made.

(vii)   This is also the appropriate opportunity to at least mentally prepare plans, decide procedures, and settle new targets and standards for next appraisal. These should be put before the employees for their careful study, analysis and try to make consensus on them.

(viii)   Always remember to include the appraisee in the review of post-appraisal reports. It will establish coordination and cooperation between the employees and the management.

10.9   Contemplations on Appraisal:

We have already talked a lot about the need to discuss the appraisal reports with the appraisee. It is essential to bring the strong and weak points of the performance of the employee to his notice. The objectives of the performance appraisal are (1) The management knows well the strong and weak points and the skills its employees possess (2) To help the management decide upon what steps it ought to take to improve its employee's performance (3) The employees get unbiased reviews of their performance whether they are following organisational objectives or not (4) If yes, how are they going to be benefitted by their good performance (5) If no, how are they going to lose. This process ought to be two-way. Until the appraisees are actively involved in it, how will they come to know what they are doing or not doing for their organisation? How will the managements come to know what difficulties their employees have been facing while performing on their jobs? How will smooth interaction take place between the policy/decision makers and their implementers? How will both understand each other? This could be possible if the employees are also taken into confidence at every level of policy/ decision making and free interaction is facilitated between them because they are the people who will implement them at the ground level. For this an environment free from hesitation is required and the managements must ensure it by following steps given below:

(i)   The post-appraisal reviews must be made in peaceful atmosphere. There should be no outside interference in it at the time of review.

(ii)   The review should be done in a cordial manner. It should not be intimidating. The appraisee should be given full opportunity to present his side unhesitatingly.

(iii)   The review should be based on self-appraisal as well as performance appraisal; and both should be thoroughly and openly discussed.

(iv)   It should also be observed when reviewing whether the job-roles, his duties and responsibilities, his commitments to organisational objectives etc. were clear to the appraisee or not.

(v)   It should also be decided whether the performance targets and agreed upon work-expectations were clear to the appraisee or not.

(vi)   It should also be judged whether the concept of good performance with reference to appraisees' job which might have made him to concentrate on it, was clear to him or not.

(vii)   Appraisal report of each area should be analysed one by one separately and seen whether the performance was in tune with already settled targets or not. If yes, how much?

(viii)   Post-appraisal remedial measures to be taken up and these ought to be discussed with the appraisee so that he is assured of his growth. It will help the appraiser and the management to win the trust of the employee.

10.10 Characteristics of Effective Appraisal:

Effective appraisals are those which:

(i)   Have targets and the standards very clear.
(ii)   Make objective, unbiased and job-centered appraisal.
(iii)   Extend timely guidance to the appraisee.
(iv)   Convey the targets, objectives and goals in clear terms.

(v)   Know well what acceptable appraisal is.

(vi)   Uses comprehensible examples and references.

(vii)   Analyses appraisal format and job-details in time and establishes a good rapport between both.

(viii) Is able to collect feedback from the appraisee also.

(ix)   Provide cordial atmosphere for appraisal so that the appraisee could put his side frankly and unhesitatingly.

(x)   Choose a single area but makes comprehensive appraisal.

(xi)   Last but the most important: Concentrates fully on appraisal procedures only. Even mobile phones should also be switched off.

10.11 Providing Feedback:

If the feedback is not immediately provided to the appraisee, the objectives of the appraisal procedure would be defeated. Maximum advantages could be garnered only if the feedback is given as early as possible. Effective feedback is that which is swift, specific, comprehensive, positive (even when shortcomings are pointed out) objective and frequent. Be it as employee or teacher or student: All wish earnestly to know how better they performed. Feedback to students has already been discussed in Chapters One and Five.

Effective feedback has some essential steps to be followed religiously by the appraiser. First step involves making the importance and objectives of the feedback very clear so that the employee concerned makes best use of it. The feedback comments ought to be very positive like: The model reading was very good. Voice was clear and audible to the last-bencher. Very clear opinion be made on how to make the feedback effective so that the appraisee understands it well and makes it part of his performance.

Under the second step, the feedback ought to be provided in simple and comprehensible words so that it looks natural. Hypothetical comments should never be made. Comments should be definite like when you were reading, your body language was in tune with reference to the context. What effects that particular behaviour o the reader-teacher had had on the audiences, must be special mentioned. Positive, creative, constructive and reformative feedb should be presented separately. No personal comments on the appraisee should be made. Feedback should be context-based only. The employee's personal characteristics should never be part of feedback. It should be quick, time bound and dignified. Late feedback is useless.

Under third step, keeping the organisational and individual goals in mind suggestions and opinions are invited about what will be next strategy. Focus is only on what is to be done next. Timely positive and encouraging feedback on excellent performance is highly desirable and most useful for both: The individual as well as the organisation. Positive feedback boosts the morale of the appraisee. So it should never be overlooked. Suggestions and appreciations should be in clear and comprehensible terms. Discussions on the feedback should be open and free. After the feedback reviews/analysis, the follow-up-meetings/sessions must be arranged and held.

The above procedure is for the appraisal made by any senior. The teachers' performance appraisal is done at several levels by different people. It ought to be and must be continued because there is no harm in it. The performance appraisal of the teachers is as much significant for the institution as it is for the students, parents in particular and the society in general. It is rather more important for the students and the parents. Therefore all schools and colleges must opt for this multiple type of appraisal of teachers. It will be a good step. Performance appraisal of teachers by the students has already been discussed in Chapters One and Five. In Chapter One, we had dwelt upon the crucial question that besides educational authorities, who should appraise the teachers. And we had concluded that it will be highly desirable and will be a revolutionary step in education sector if the students and parents are also given this right and opportunity as they are the principal stakeholders. It will certainly contain the fast deteriorating image of the teachers and the educational institutions in the society.

Sooner this is adopted; the better it will be for the teachers and the institutions in particular and the society in general. Yes, it will be fruitful if a joint session of the school authorities, parents and the students is held in which educational, moral and social goals of the institution should be clearly spelled out for (1) all work together for their achievement (2) the parents and the students are very well aware of what they have to assess while appraising their teachers showing due respects to the latter and are fully prepared to perform this important function. After all, performance appraisal is not a child's play.

❏❏❏❏

CHAPTER 11
Continuous Performance Monitoring

Performance appraisal is not one day process. It is a continuous process and it ought to be continued to gain maximum benefits out of this exercise. When it goes on continuously, its thorough check-up which is one of its major part should also be kept going. Appraisal is absolutely a formal process which is done after an already decided time gap. Informal but very important and continuous part of this process is its day to day check-up which the managements get it done through its senior and experienced personnel.

Inspection of the employees' work and conduct, continuous interaction between the appraiser and the appraisee in case of any shortcomings in his performance, appreciation of good performance and the suggestions/guidance for improvement in average performance: are day to day appraisal activities which we notice daily and might have experienced formally or informally at any stage of our career. The truth is that this informal appraisal is more important not only for the employee but the organisation also. Being informal, it teaches the employees more than the formal ones which are held periodically in highly artificial manners. The former establishes a smooth rapport between the employees and the day to day appraiser. Most of the important skills/things are passed on from the experienced to inexperienced ones just through informal interaction. In formal appraisals the appraiser may try to be informal during the periodical appraisal even then this process smells of evaluation and inspection by an authority. But it is not so with the day to day monitoring of the work and guidance to the needy by an experienced senior person of the organisation. That is why this informal appraisal process leaves a permanent, positive and indelible impression on the minds of employees' leading to good performance. This procedure is almost the same as the teacher applies daily in the class to monitor the activities of his students and improve their reading-learning skills but evaluates them quarterly/

half-yearly to test their memory retention and yearly for promotion to the next class. It is right that the students are promoted to the next class on the basis of written tests but it is equally true that the students are evaluated daily orally or by observation which is no less important. The scheme of Continuous Comprehensive Evaluation introduced by the Central Board of Education Delhi is carried out on the basis of daily monitoring of students' academic/ co-curricular activities.

11.1   Advantages and Disadvantages of Continuous Performance Monitoring:

The greatest advantage of continuous appraisal is that the problems coming in the way of performance can be quickly sorted out on daily basis thus helping the performer go ahead with his job without any obstacles. It is true and correct to some extent that the performer hesitates in discussing the problems that he faces in his daily functioning and at times even desists to speak about them fearing humiliations among the peers. He fears lest his superior or colleagues start making a fun of him saying he cannot do such a petty job. Day to day observation and appraisal helps the appraiser to notice himself what problems the employees have been facing and comes forward to extend help or guidance. Yes, continuous appraisal has a few disadvantages also. And these are: (1) sometimes the appraiser starts interfering without any need. It may be due to his dominant nature or over activeness thus poking his nose when not needed at all. It kills the initiatives of the employees (2) the appraiser has faith in none except himself. He does not believe that his inexperienced young workforce can perform well without his guidance/help. Thus he volunteers the help/guidance when it is least needed (3) it also violates the employees' rights of self-decision making.

If the appraiser keeps control over his overindulgence, then the day-to-day performance monitoring could be the best for individual professional growth and development of the organisation. Therefore the supervisors ought to keep their overbearing nature under control. These shortcomings will be least or not at all found in the appraisers who are experts in this art. They extend guidance/help only when it is needed most.

11.2   Problem Solving during Continuous Performance Monitoring:

Problem solving by day-to-day monitoring is a very easy and convenient process which needs to be adopted by those appraisers who want to see actual and natural professional development of the employees as well as the institution. For this the appraiser needs to be expert in close observation, sense the difficulties the employees might be experiencing and analyse them on the spot. Therefore the appraiser ought to stay on his toes but without indulging in overbearing actions mentioned above, and extend his help and guidance whenever most needed by the employees being appraised and solve their problems then and there.

(i)   Discrepancy Statement:

This process involves identifying the problems, going into their roots, understanding them, analyzing their causes, then suggesting ways and means to solve them and then see whether his suggestions are being followed and implemented or not. The appraiser will have to rely on his own observation in this regard and not to blindly believe what is reported to him by others. May be the problem was exaggerated or may not actually be in existence: For example the problems of pronunciation in a teacher from the North-Eastern region. It is well known that regional influences on pronunciation are quite prominent. Kindly refer to the humorous example of a Bihar teacher quoted earlier in Chapter 10. Though the pronunciation was inappropriate but that did not make him a bad performer in teaching. We cannot label him a bad teacher or his teaching ineffective just because of his wrong utterances of any sound which he could improve gradually by practice when pointed out, helped and guided properly by the appraiser or any of his colleagues. The management of educational institutions must hold special training for such teachers if any in their institutions. In order to identifying problems in the performance the appraiser needs to see:

   (a) Whether the performance is up to expectations or not?
   (b) What are the reasons of low spirits?
   (c) Is there much difference in expected performance and the actual one?
   (d) Is this gap causing concern in the organisation?
   (e) Can this problem be sorted out by re-training or re-orientation?

(ii) Significance of Discrepancy:

The appraiser should never hesitate in analyzing how much harmful the discrepancy in question could be for the organisation. In order to fix this question, these questions could be helpful:

(a) Why is the discrepancy significant?
(b) Is the resolution of the discrepancy necessary?
(c) If not resolved what can be the consequences?
(d) Is the solution to the problem possible?
(e) Can the problem be ignored?

(iii) Root Cause of the Discrepancy:

The appraiser should study the problem carefully and try to find out the root causes of the same. Is it due to the lack of performance skills? It may be that the appraisee knowingly is causing the discrepancies due to extraneous reasons or he might be not able to perform in spite of his best efforts and willpower. In such situations the following questions may help the appraiser:

(a) Can the employee perform if he so desires?
(b) If no, can this unwillingness affect his livelihood?
(c) If he can, is he shirking his job?
(d) Is he skilled to do the particular job?

(iv) Causes of Skill Deficiency:

May be that the employee did the job in the past but is unable to do the same now due to any genuine reason like forgetfulness, physical or mental handicaps or due to long time gap between his former performance and the present. In such situations it will be just wastage of time if he is sent for retraining. So the appraiser should look for answers to the following questions:

(a) Was the employee successful in doing the same job earlier?
(b) Was regular feedback given on his performance?
(c) If yes, is there too much time gap between the past and present performances?

(d) If yes, could regular feedback on his present performance help him improve and come up to the past standards?

(e) If no, is there any need to provide retraining to him?

(v)   In the Event of Irregular Performance:

May be that the employee neither got the opportunity to do that particular job regularly or at short intervals nor got the timely and regular feedback? In such circumstances the following questions may help the appraiser:

(a) Did the employee get fair opportunities to practise on that particular job?

(b) If yes, was timely feedback provided to him?

(c) If no, how he got to know about his performance standards?

(vi)   In the Absence of Timely Feedback:

May be the employee continued practising or working on that particular job but timely and regular feedback was not provided to him keeping him in dark about his performance standards and depriving him of proper guidance for improvement in his performance. In such situations the following questions may help the appraiser:

(a) Was the employee able to get the right information about his performance standards or not?

(b) Could that information be equaled to feedback?

(c) If yes, was the employee told in clear words how he could improve his performance?

(d) Was the employee able to understand those suggestions?

(e) Did he follow those suggestions?

(f) Was this information passed onto him just after his performance?

(vii)   Employee's State of Mind:

May be that the employee is under stress due to some domestic problem or hostile environment at the workplace and is unable to concentrate on his job. The following questions may help the appraiser to know the reasons for his poor performance:

(a) Is the environment at the workplace cordial?
(b) If no, what the organisation/department can do to make the environment employee friendly?
(c) If yes, is the employee under stress due to any domestic reason/problem?
(d) If yes, how he could be relieved of the stress/anxiety?
(e) Can the organisation/department do anything to help him out of the domestic problem or to boost his morale?

(viii) Lack of Interest in Desired Performance:

May be that the job assigned to him is not of his taste or interests or beyond his working capacity or he is considering the assigned job as a punishment to him or taking it as a burden. The following queries may help the appraiser under such situations:

(a) Is the employee taking due interest in the job?
(b) Did the employee ever request to exempt him from that particular job?
(c) If no, what could be any other reason for poor performance?
(d) Is the particular job like a punishment to the employee?

(ix) Delight from Poor Performance:

It has also been seen that sometimes the employees shirk their jobs intentionally to tease or challenge their superiors and seek enjoyment through such adamant behaviour. Such behaviour is more prominent among those employees who are actively associated with workers' unions. They like to go against the establishment because it looks more revolutionary and satisfying to them. Sometimes they wish to establish models for other workers to follow. Another possibility could be that the employee expects more favours from his poor performance as seen sometimes that the organisations shower favours on undeserving employees due to pressures from outside forces. The appraiser may pose the following questions to analyse the situation in a better way:

(a) Is the employee closely connected to any workers' union?
(b) Can the employee get any favour for his poor performance?

(c) Does the employee feel great after his poor performance?

(d) Does the employee get any special attention or emulation or any special place after his poor performance?

(e) Does the management reward poor performance ignoring good performers due to any extraneous reason?

(x)   Hurdles in good performance:

Sometimes good performers face practical difficulties at the workplace. He may be getting confused/troubled by disturbances or is not equipped with necessary equipments/tools or may be facing shortage of time or mental disturbance on account of his domestic reasons or hostile atmosphere at the work-place. In such situations, the following questions may help the appraiser:

(a) Are there any hurdles before the employee which block his good performance?

(b) Can the performance be improved if these hurdles are removed or reduced?

(c) Is the employee aware what is expected of him?

(d) Does the employee know when, where and what job he has to do?

(e) Does the employee have ample time for good performance?

(f) Has the employee the desired liberty to take his independent decisions to perform well if the need arises?

(g) Can the reduction of workload on the employee improve his performance?

(h) Could the performance be improved by removing causes of maladministration?

(xi)   Disinterest in Good Performance:

Sometimes the employee loses interests in his job when he finds that good performance gets no appreciation whereas the poor ones get rewards. Under such circumstances, the mindset of the employee needs probing and the following questions may help the appraiser:

(a) Why does the employee perform well in spite of being ignored?

(b) Does the employee consider good performance necessary in his professional development?

(c) Does the good performer get any positive motivation for doing well?

(d) Does the employee get inner satisfaction by his good performance?

(e) Does the employee feel great after his good performance?

(f) Does good performance place an employee in better position among his peers or in the organisation?

(g) Does good performance meet an employee's needs well?

(h) Does a performer get undesirable results on account of his average performance?

11.3 Conclusion:

Appraising and managing appraisal are different things. Management of appraisal is as difficult as doing appraisal. The biggest problem that arises in a successful and effective appraisal is maintaining its objectivity. As anyone gets an authority, dictatorship which is the greatest enemy of objectivity, creeps in automatically.

When is appraisal to be made, who to be appraised and by whom the particular job (of appraisal) has to be done are very crucial and have to be decided in advance.

Besides this, which department will be given this important duty to ensure that all appraisal work goes on smoothly, which department will keep the records safely and up to which term such documents need to be preserved? In most of the organisations, this job is normally done by the Human Resource Department. Though realising its importance some institutions have started establishing HR Departments still most of the educational institutions do not have such department. So the principal and his administrative staff are the best preservers of such documents and most institutions do so.

Besides the above the management will have to ensure the performance appraisal of each of the employees at regular intervals on the basis of set standards and see that their performance continues improving unabated. Performance appraisal is a continuous comprehensive exercise which ought to be carried out in a systemat and classified manner and each of the employees needs to under it not only for his individual professional development but for the betterment of the organisation also. It is an established norm that performance appraisal should be done as many times as it is considered necessary. It depends on employee to employee. For example, the experienced employees do not need the appraisal as frequently as the new and inexperienced ones may. But the employee being considered for the appraisal must be informed in advance. Similarly the feedback needs to be provided just after the appraisal or as early as possible in which he should be informed in comprehensible terms whether his performance is as per expectations or not; and if not how can he improve it.

Performance appraisal is the responsibility of the management. It should be held under its set policies, established methods and mutually agreed upon procedures. Later the results of the appraisal must be jointly discussed in a cordial manner. The appraiser and the management has also to decide whether there is any need for retraining or for holding workshops for further improvement or not. The management should never be sticking only to one method of appraisal. It ought to be open and suitable to times, place and other conditions. The procedure should be absolutely transparent. It is true that BARS (Behaviourally Anchored Rating Scale) and MBO (Management by Objectives) are more popular these days. But what have we to do with popularity? If none of these two is suitable to our institution, then we must opt for the one which is favoured by the majority. The management should take decision judiciously in this regard and all the employees should be informed about it well in advance. There may a debate in this regard if need arises or the management wants to involve all the employees which would be a good step to win the trust of the entire team.

The employees need to know very well what appraisal means, how it will be done and what is its importance for them from their professional point of view and for the organisation. It will be timely to mention here that the management must set standards for excellent and acceptable performance and come forward as role models. It will help in the achievement of the organisational goals. But it should also not forget that each of the employees has his individual professional goals which made him to join a particular organisation.

It is the duty of the management to see that their individual goals are achieved first because if the employees stay satisfied, it will be the parent organisation which will ultimately benefit from the contented employees. At least there should a balance between both the objectives otherwise its own organisational objectives will be in danger.

Most of the managements are informally cautious about the performance of the employee as he comes at the time of interview to be selected and join their organisation and they ought to be because once the employee joins, he becomes a liability. Therefore, his qualifications, experience, skills he is equipped with, his general behaviour and his suitability to the organisation ought to be minutely studied. This step is very important. Undoubtedly the formal appraisal starts after the employee joins and sets on his professional journey in the new setting and decides how he has to achieve the organisational goals at the earliest. The management must define the goals very clearly. The goals should be attainable. They should be measurable. Such objectives themselves motivate the employees as these are simple and well comprehensible. The objectives should be revised at regular intervals. Continuous process of the appraisal helps in establishing performance standards. Measurable objectives and objective appraisals improve performance and are welcome by the employees because they are comprehensible, definite, real and quantified.

Where the managements are sincere with the appraisal schemes, the employees are bound to be responsive and accountable as it keeps them charged with positive energies. They understand their work-responsibilities well and proceed to perform accordingly. They plan their work style from the very beginning in such a manner that leads them to the achievement of their targets: Individual as well as organisational. The management must ensure availability of all facilities, timely and proper guidance and cordial environment to their employees at the workplace which are necessary for their better performance and achievement of the goals.

Most important is self-appraisal. The managements ought to t their employees in this art and motivate them to start this he practice. All help and guidance should be given to the employees in this regard. The managements and the appraisers should also ensure that the errors related to appraisal like "Lack of objectivity" and "Halo error" does not creep in the system.

The managements ought to take all necessary steps which ensure smooth and successful appraisal procedures. Work-expectations, targets and the background of the employee needs to be reviewed regularly, preparation of the employee for self-appraisal, evaluation of work-expectations and actual performance, preparing of notes on the appraisal, deliberations and analysis of the employee's expected professional development, providing regular and timely feedback, joint deliberations on the appraisal results and preparing the final appraisal report, further discussions with the seniors, organisational development are the most prominent areas which ought to be continuously monitored. This procedure should be in writing to meet legal necessities if situation arises and copies of the relevant records should immediately be given to the concerned employee as well.

Last but not the least important is the fact that training is part and parcel of the appraisal system which continues incessantly. The employees not only need reorientation but up to date knowledge also in the fast changing scenario. The managements should never ignore this. Appraisal ought to be employee-centered which will be for the good of both: Employees and the organisation.

❑❑❑❑

CHAPTER 12

Performance Appraisal Forms

We have dealt with a serious and very important topic like performance appraisal deeply and comprehensively. During these deliberations we also dwelt on when, how, why and who should make performance appraisal so as to make its best use. We focused on the teachers' performance appraisal and discussed it from all angles. Everyone who has a stake in the matter has a right to appraise the performance. Education is one of such areas with which several segments of the society are not only directly related but affected also. Among them are educational institutions/education department as well as the students and the parents. Therefore we have prepared performance appraisal forms for each which could be used to appraise the teachers.

One thing ought to be made clear. These pro forma are modifiable as per needs of time, place and other situations. The institutions can make changes in them or add more if the need arises. These pro forma could be used advantageously for the appraisal of teachers working in schools, colleges and universities. These are easy to use, based on appraisal principles, are transparent, will promote cooperation, are development oriented, quality improving and set the appraisal standards. We hope that these pro forma could appraise the teachers from the community development points of view and facilitate fast social change. Feedback from the readers/users will be welcome.

The appraisers will also have to be careful when using these pro forma because the utility of tools and equipments depends more on the skills of the users. They should utilize these pro forma for teacher-centric purposes like their educational, professional and individual development because the institutional development in particular and social development in general solely depends on the teachers' contentment levels. But it does not mean that they sta ignoring the performance appraisal policies. They must be firm in implementation of appraisal policies otherwise the whole exercise may turn to be counter-effective. It is essential that the teachers appraisal is done very honestly after due discussions with them lest the organisational/institutional problems start cropping up. Though the list given below of what the appraiser should do and what not, is just indicative still it may make the things quite clear about it:

12.1   Suggestions regarding Appraisal:

What ought to be done?	What not to be done?
1. Fix the goals before going for appraisal. 2. Appraise on the basis of sufficient knowledge. 3. Include relevant areas only in the appraisal. 4. Appraise job-related performance only. 5. Appraise only in an objective manner. 6. Take the appraisee in your confidence before commencing upon the appraisal process.	7. Do not appraise aimlessly. 8. Do not appraise without sufficient knowledge. 9. Never include irrelevant areas in the appraisal. 10. Never include personal traits of the appraisee in the appraisal. 11. Never permit subjectivity to creep in the appraisal. 12. Never create fear, anxiety or suspicions in the mind of the appraisee.

These moral responsibilities will automatically be fulfilled when these pro forma are used for appraisal because these are capable of collecting qualitative and quantitative information about the performance of the teachers.

12.2 Performance Appraisal Proformas:

Appendix 1
Fortnightly Self-appraisal by the Teachers

Teacher's name_____ Session_____ Appraisal cycle_____

— Note: Please encircle the grade you deem applicable to you. Be honest.

1. My Previous fortnight's goals:

Class	Subject	Lesson	CW/HW/Projects/Experience and CC Activities

2. The Goals I achieved:

Class	Subject	Lesson	CW/HW/Projects/Experience and CC Activities

3. More CC Activities I facilitated:

C L A S S	Subject	Projects/Experiments/ Models/Fine Arts/ Performing Arts etc.

4.   Homework Monitoring:

5.   Book I read during this fortnight/month:

Title of the book

Writer's name

Brief Gist/Summary

6.   Introduced to the students (If no, why?)

7.   Subject Related Problems That I Put in this Month's Faculty Meeting:

Problem in Brief :

Solution Suggested:

8.   Wall-Magazine Contributions from each class:

9. Steps Taken for development of Language Skills
(Essential for all teachers)

Reading	
Writing	
Listening	
Speaking	

10. My Behaviour in the Class   Grading (Please encircle the grade)

		Always	Very often	Often	Never
1.	Particular about teacher like appearance.	4	3	2	1
2.	Enter the class smilingly and wish students.	4	3	2	1
3.	Check the absentees from roll-call book or roll-call quickly.	4	3	2	1
4.	Commence with the teaching without wasting time.	4	3	2	1
5.	Keep taking rounds to supervise.	4	3	2	1
6.	Check if any student is without book.	4	3	2	1
7.	Come prepared with the lesson.	4	3	2	1
8.	Follow the lesson plan strictly.	4	3	2	1
9.	Use of topic-related humorous incidents/ anecdotes etc. to make the teaching lively.	4	3	2	1
10.	Prefer appropriate role-play while teaching.	4	3	2	1
11.	Facilitate understanding of the concepts.	4	3	2	1
12.	Write down difficult words/concepts on the blackboard.	4	3	2	1
13.	Encourage students to ask questions.	4	3	2	1
14.	Ask probing question while teaching.	4	3	2	1
15.	Maintain eye contact with the students.	4	3	2	1
16.	Homework checking.	4	3	2	1
17.	Errors are neatly written on the margins of note-books.	4	3	2	1
18.	Follow-up-work on errors is insisted.	4	3	2	1
19.	Regularly check the follow-up-work.	4	3	2	1
20.	Ensure the parents sign the note-books.	4	3	2	1
21.	Students' diary is regularly checked.	4	3	2	1
22.	Classroom regulations defined.	4	3	2	1

23. Promote self-discipline in the classroom.	4	3	2	1
24. Use of Audio-Visual Aids.	4	3	2	1
25. Promote subject related co-curricular activities.	4	3	2	1
26. Give a few minutes daily for development of personal hygiene among students.	4	3	2	1
27. Every month I read a book of students' level and introduce it to them.	4	3	2	1
28. General attitude towards student.	4	3	2	1
29. Compliance of 3-minutes switch over rule.	4	3	2	1
30. Regularity to attending the school.	4	3	2	1
31. Punctuality to assigned duties.	4	3	2	1
32. Readiness to extra work in the school.	4	3	2	1
33. Dynamism in faculty meetings.	4	3	2	1
34. Dynamism for moral education.	4	3	2	1
35. Relationship with colleagues.	4	3	2	1
36. Relationship with the Vice-Principal.	4	3	2	1
37. Relationship with the Head.	4	3	2	1
Total Score of Item 1 to 37				

Signature of the Appraiser_____   Signature of Teacher_____

Comments by the Principal_____

Manager_____

Appendix 2
Proforma For Performance Appraisal Of Teachers By Students

Name of Teacher Ms/Mr_____ Subject_____

— Note:Please encircle the number you deem fit in response of each statement.

Teacher's Behaviour Statements	Rating			
	Always	Very often	Often	Never
1. Enters the class with a smiling face.	4	3	2	1
2. Reciprocates the students' wishes well.	4	3	2	1
3. Has a very sweet and charming voice.	4	3	2	1
4. Presents the topic clearly and logically.	4	3	2	1
5. Helps the students grasp the topic well.	4	3	2	1
6. Is fully audible.	4	3	2	1
7. Presents his material intelligibly.	4	3	2	1
8. Maintains continuity in the teaching.	4	3	2	1
9. Has command over his subject.	4	3	2	1
10. Explains the terms and concepts very clearly.	4	3	2	1
11. Encourages the students to put questions.	4	3	2	1
12. Furnishes extra relevant information not available in the book.	4	3	2	1
13. Makes use of all the available teaching aids like charts, models, slides, films etc.	4	3	2	1
14. Maintains comfortable pace in the teaching.	4	3	2	1
15. Is apt and concise.	4	3	2	1
16. Gives appropriate and relevant examples and illustrations.	4	3	2	1
17. Does not waste on time-filling trivial talks during teaching.	4	3	2	1
18. Stimulates the students to think analytically.	4	3	2	1
19. Does not ridicule the students' wrong or inappropriate answers.	4	3	2	1
20. Gives moderate home-work.	4	3	2	1
21. Is meticulous in checking our homework.	4	3	2	1
22. Fills up the students with enthusiasm for his subject.	4	3	2	1

23.	Equips the students with latest knowledge in his subject.	4	3	2	1
24.	Makes the students aware about the objectives of teaching the topic.	4	3	2	1
25.	Welcomes students' viewpoints on the topic being taught.	4	3	2	1
26.	Has a good sense of humour.	4	3	2	1
27.	Welcomes concept-related good jokes.	4	3	2	1
28.	Quite often uses concept-related humour while teaching and makes the teaching very interesting.	4	3	2	1
29.	Uses the blackboard frequently to make the tough concepts clear.	4	3	2	1
30.	Has very good command over languages.	4	3	2	1
31.	Has a good vocabulary.	4	3	2	1
32.	Writes on the blackboard legibly.	4	3	2	1
33.	Is skilled in drawing diagrams and figures on the blackboard.	4	3	2	1
34.	Plans the blackboard summary very well in small notes.	4	3	2	1
35.	Trains us in note-making using his art of note-making on the blackboards.	4	3	2	1
36.	Feels at confident while teaching.	4	3	2	1
37.	Commands faith and respect among students.	4	3	2	1
38.	Maintains peace and discipline in the classroom.	4	3	2	1
39.	Has a sympathetic attitude towards all students.	4	3	2	1
40.	Has more sympathetic attitude towards needy students.	4	3	2	1
41.	Is the most sympathetic to differently abled students.	4	3	2	1
42.	Is very friendly with the students.	4	3	2	1
43.	Appreciates the students' accomplishments.	4	3	2	1
44.	Appears as if enjoys teaching very much.	4	3	2	1
45.	Teaches upto the points and avoids overdosing.	4	3	2	1
46.	Introduces relevant reference books to the students.	4	3	2	1

47. Is polite but in firm.	4	3	2	1
48. Deals us with democratic approach.	4	3	2	1
49. Avoids deviating from good mannerisms.	4	3	2	1
50. Has a sharp memory.	4	3	2	1
51. Teaches us how to develop memory.	4	3	2	1
52. Which teacher you like most?	4	3	2	1
53. Why do you like this teacher most?	Smt/Sh:			
54. What subject she/he teaches you?				
55. Is she/he equally popular among other students?	Yes	No		
	Yes	No		
Total of 1 to 51 :				

Brief Note about 52 to 55 by the Vice Principal/Principal:

Vice-Principal

Teacher's Signatures   Principal

Appendix 3
Proforma For Performance Appraisal Of Teachers

(Model 1)

Directions: Please rate   (5) as superior,   (4) Strong   (3) Average   (2) Fair   (1) Poor

Behaviour Statements	Rating			
	Always	Very often	Often	Never
1. Develops short range goals.	4	3	2	1
2. Exercises emotional stability.	4	3	2	1
3. Prepares daily lesson plans.	4	3	2	1
4. Includes objectives, key questions, and reinforcement strategies in lesson plans.	4	3	2	1
5. Is creative and flexible.	4	3	2	1
6. Plans as per needs of the individual students.	4	3	2	1
7. Knows subject matter well.	4	3	2	1
A. Teaching Skills				
8. Provides for individual differences.	4	3	2	1
9. Uses basic skills effectively.	4	3	2	1
10. Objectively evaluates students' progress.	4	3	2	1
11. Asks questions well in easy to understand words.	4	3	2	1
12. Backs up the students.	4	3	2	1
13. Praises the students.	4	3	2	1
14. Encourages the students.	4	3	2	1
15. Implements innovative techniques.	4	3	2	1
16. Encourages students' self-discipline.	4	3	2	1
17. Provides challenging and facilitative atmosphere.	4	3	2	1
18. Exhibits effective speech patterns.	4	3	2	1
19. Provides effective time on task.	4	3	2	1
20. Maintains rapport with the students.	4	3	2	1

B. **Professional Attitude**	4	3	2	1
21. Works well with peers.	4	3	2	1
22. Assumes responsibility.	4	3	2	1
23. Reacts favorably to positive and constructive criticism.	4	3	2	1
24. Seeks professional growth.	4	3	2	1
25. Keeps excellent records.	4	3	2	1
26. Is punctual.	4	3	2	1
27. Is regular in school.	4	3	2	1
28. Attends meetings regularly.	4	3	2	1
29. Is willing to adapt to new changes.	4	3	2	1
30. Keeps abreast of curriculum and instruction.	4	3	2	1
31. Observes professional ethics.	4	3	2	1
32. Demonstrates pride in his work.	4	3	2	1
33. Exhibits continuing interest in the students.	4	3	2	1
34. Encourages parents' interest.	4	3	2	1
C. **Personal Characteristics**				
35. Radiates enthusiasm.	4	3	2	1
36. Uses sound judgement.	4	3	2	1
37. Dresses meticulously.	4	3	2	1
38. Grooms appropriately.	4	3	2	1
39. Demonstrates integrity.	4	3	2	1
40. Demonstrates leadership skills.	4	3	2	1
41. Demonstrates democratic values.	4	3	2	1
42. Shows a sense of humour.	4	3	2	1
43. Promotes Creativity	4	3	2	1
44. Arouses Analytical Thinking	4	3	2	1
45. Promotes Cordiality.	4	3	2	1

Total from 1 to 45
Comments by the Appraiser:
Signature of the Teacher:

Signature of the Manager:

Appendix 4
Proforma For Performance Appraisal Of Teachers

(Model 2)

Note: Rating values   (5) Superior,   (4) Strong   (3) Average   (2) Fair   (1) Poor

Behaviour Statements Grades: Please encircle the grade you deem fit

Grades	Always	Very often	Often	Never
1. Lesson Planning	1	2	3	4
2. Clarity of Lesson Purpose	1	2	3	4
3. Lesson Presentation	1	2	3	4
4. Classroom Organisation	1	2	3	4
5. Co-curricular activities.	1	2	3	4
6. Pupil Involvement	1	2	3	4
7. Teacher-Pupil Rapport	1	2	3	4
8. Classroom Management	1	2	3	4
9. Questioning Skills	1	2	3	4
10. Students' Response to Qs	1	2	3	4
11. Acceptance of Students' answers	1	2	3	4
12. Teacher Dynamism	1	2	3	4
13. Student-Centredness of the Lessons	1	2	3	4
14. Mastery of Subject Matter	1	2	3	4
15. Appropriateness of the matter.	1	2	3	4
16. Class-work Management	1	2	3	4
17. Homework Management	1	2	3	4
18. Follow-up-Work Monitoring	1	2	3	4
19. Teacher Appearance	1	2	3	4
20. General Attitude towards students.	1	2	3	4
21. Teacher-Parents Rapport	1	2	3	4
22. Use of relevant anecdotes	1	2	3	4
23. Audibility to the Class	1	2	3	4
24. Students' Attention Seeking Behaviour	1	2	3	4
25. Students' Participation Seeking Behaviour	1	2	3	4
26. Use of Black Board	1	2	3	4
27. Use of Audio-Visual Aids	1	2	3	4

28. Role Model of the Teacher	1	2	3	4
29. Reads reference books	1	2	3	4
30. Introduces Them to Students	1	2	3	4
31. Use of Germane Humour	1	2	3	4
32. Readiness to Extra Duties	1	2	3	4
33. Arouses Creative Thinking	1	2	3	4
34. Arouses Analytical Thinking	1	2	3	4
35. Promotes Cordiality	1	2	3	4

Total of 1 to 35

Comments by the Appraiser:

Signature of Teacher:

Signature of Manager:

Appendix 5
Proforma For Performance Appraisal By Education Department

District:_____   Date_____

1. Name of the Teacher: Ms/Mr._____
2. Designation_____
3. School/College:_____
4. Class inspected_____
5. Subject Taught_____
6. Class Strength:_____   Students Present_____
7. OBSERVATION REPORT   Grades

	4	3	2	1
• Lesson Planning	4	3	2	1
• Clarity of Lesson Purpose	4	3	2	1
• Lesson Presentation	4	3	2	1
• Classroom Organisation	4	3	2	1
• Use of AV Aids.	4	3	2	1
• Pupil Involvement	4	3	2	1
• Teacher-Pupil Rapport	4	3	2	1
• Classroom Management	4	3	2	1
• Questioning Skills	4	3	2	1
• Students' Response to Qs	4	3	2	1
• Acceptance of Students' answers	4	3	2	1
• Teacher Dynamism	4	3	2	1
• Student-Centredness of the Lesson	4	3	2	1
• Mastery of Subject Matter	4	3	2	1
• Appropriateness of the matter.	4	3	2	1
• Class-work Management	4	3	2	1
• Homework Management	4	3	2	1
• Follow-up-Work Monitoring	4	3	2	1
• Correlation with Earlier Knowledge	4	3	2	1
• General Attitude towards students.	4	3	2	1
• Teacher-students Rapport	4	3	2	1
• Use of relevant anecdotes	4	3	2	1
• Audibility to the Class	4	3	2	1
• Attention Seeking Behaviour	4	3	2	1
• Gives Additional Knowledge	4	3	2	1
• Use of Blackboard	4	3	2	1
• Role Model of the Teacher	4	3	2	1

• Reads reference books	4	3	2	1
• Introduces Them to Students	4	3	2	1
• Use of Germane Humour	4	3	2	1
• Helps weak students	4	3	2	1
• Arouses Creative Thinking	4	3	2	1
• Arouses Analytical Thinking	4	3	2	1
• Promotes Cordiality	4	3	2	1
Teacher's appearance	4	3	2	1

Total of 1 to 35

General Remarks/Suggestions:

Signatures of the Observer

Signatures of the Teacher

Report Discussed With_____

Appendix 6
Proforma For Performance Appraisal Of University Teachers

Note: Rating values   (5) Superior,   (4) Strong   (3) Average   (2) Fair   (1) Poor

1.   Name Mr/Mrs. _____
2.   Date of Birth _____
3.   Date of joining _____
4.   Joined as _____
5.   Present Designation _____
6.   Total Experience _____
7.   Any other details you wish to give _____
8.   Details ofthe Academic Qualifications

Examination Passed	Year	Div/Gd	College/University
1. Matric			
2. Sr. Sec.			
3. First Degree			
4. PG Degree			
5. PG Diploma			
6. M.Phil.			
7. Ph.D.			
8. Post.Doctoral			
9. Any other			
10. Any more			

9.   Details of the Academic Achievements

S.No	Level	Sponsoring Agency	State	National	International
1	Primary				
2	Secondary				
3	Sr. Sec.				
4	1st Degree				
5	P.G.				
6	M.Phil.				
7	Ph.D.				
8	Any other				

10.   Details of any Other/Additional Qualification if any

S. No	Year	Name of Qualification	Authority	Specializartion
1				
2				

11.   Details of any Training in Research.

S. No	Name of Institution	Course	Year	From	To
1					
2					

12.   Details of Research Experience.

S. No	Research Level	Title of Research Work	University
1	Master		
2	M.Phil		
3	Ph.D		
4	Post-Doctoral		
5	Any other		

13.   Specialization in:

S. No	Area	Contribution
1		
2		
3		

14.   Details of Research Experience.

S. No	Institution	Post	Status	Classes	From	To
1						
2						
3						
4						

15.   Details of the Scholarships/Fellowships awarded

S. No	Scholarship Fellowship	From	To	Name of the Instituition which Awarded it
1				
2				
3				

16.   Details of the Scholarships/Fellowships awarded

S. No	From	To	Amount	Funding Agency

17.   Details of Research Papers Publishes.

S. No	Title of the Paper	Theme	Journal's Name	Date, Volume and Issue

18.   Details of Seminars, Conferences or any other such symposia attended.

S. No	Topic of the Conference	Place	From	To
1				
2				
3				

19.   Details of Seminars/conferences organized

S. No	Topic of the Conference	Place	From	To
1				
2				
3				
4				

20.   Details of Books published.

S. No	Title	Year	Name of Publisher/Address

21.   Details of the Copyrights/Patents.

S. No	Name of Work	Year	Importance of the work

22. Details of Membership of Professional/Social organizations.

S. No	Name of Organisation	Status	Since

23. Visits abroad for Academic Objectives.

S. No	Country	Sponsorer	Duration	Achievements

24. Honours, Awards, Fellowships if any:

S. No	Given by	For	Status of:

25. Administrative or Managerial Experience:

S. No	Full info. of Institution	As	Duties	Achievements

26. Participation in Other Areas:

S. No	Area	As	Achievements

27.   Participation in Evaluation jobs

S. No	Area	Comments if any
1	Course Programme	
2	Home Assignments	
3	Paper Setting	
4	Invigilation	
5	I/C Exams	
6	Internal Evaluation	
7	University Evaluation	
8	Thesis/Dissertation	
9	Teaching Methods	
10	Any Other	

28.   Innovations:

S. No	Area	Comments if any
1	Curriculum	
2	Teaching Methods	
3	Appraisal Methods	
4	Exam. Evaluation.	
5	Experiments	
6	Remedial Steps	
7	Counseling	
8	Teaching Aids	
9	Memory Growth	
10	Social Cohesion	
11	Any Other	

29.   Self-Appraisal by the Teacher:

S. No	Area	Grades					Reason for Awarding this Grade
1	Teaching	A	B	C	D	E	
2	Research	A	B	C	D	E	
3	Examinations	A	B	C	D	E	
4	Evaluation	A	B	C	D	E	
5	Field Activities	A	B	C	D	E	
6	Counseling	A	B	C	D	E	
7	Consultancy	A	B	C	D	E	
8	Innovations	A	B	C	D	E	
9	Specialization	A	B	C	D	E	
10	Publications	A	B	C	D	E	
11	Affln with Profsnl. Bodies	A	B	C	D	E	
12	Experimentation	A	B	C	D	E	
13	Any other	A	B	C	D	E	

30.   Appraisal by the Appraiser:

S. No	Area	Grades					Reason for Awarding this Grade
1	Teaching	A	B	C	D	E	
2	Research	A	B	C	D	E	
3	Examinations	A	B	C	D	E	
4	Evaluation	A	B	C	D	E	
5	Field Activities	A	B	C	D	E	
6	Counseling	A	B	C	D	E	
7	Consultancy	A	B	C	D	E	
8	Innovations	A	B	C	D	E	
9	Specialization	A	B	C	D	E	
10	Publications	A	B	C	D	E	
11	Affln with Profsnl. Bodies	A	B	C	D	E	
12	Experimentation	A	B	C	D	E	
13	Any other	A	B	C	D	E	

Signature of the Teacher _____   Signature of Appraiser _____

30.   Appraisal by the Vice-Chancellor:

S. No	Area	Grades					Reason for Awarding this Grade
1	Teaching	A	B	C	D	E	
2	Research	A	B	C	D	E	
3	Examinations	A	B	C	D	E	
4	Evaluation	A	B	C	D	E	
5	Field Activities	A	B	C	D	E	
6	Counseling	A	B	C	D	E	
7	Consultancy	A	B	C	D	E	
8	Innovations	A	B	C	D	E	
9	Specialization	A	B	C	D	E	
10	Publications	A	B	C	D	E	
11	Affln with Profsnl. Bodies	A	B	C	D	E	
12	Experimentation	A	B	C	D	E	
13	Any other	A	B	C	D	E	

Signature of the VC _____

BIBLIOGRAPHY

1. Basu, M.K. (1998) Managerial Performance Appraisal in India. New Delhi: Vision Books.

2. Bhardwaj, K.S. (1988) Humour in Classroom. Guwahati: Omsons Publications.

3. Bloom B.S. (1964) Taxonomy of Educational Objectives. New York: David and Mckay.

4. Bridges, D., Elliott, J and Klass, C. (1986) Performance Appraisal as Naturalistic Inquiry: A Report on the 4th Cambridge Conference on Educational Evaluation. Cambridge Journal of Education, 16 (3): 221-233.

5. Brown, R.D. (1988) Performance Appraisal as a Tool for Staff Development. San Francisco: Jossey Bass.

6. Darling, H. (1990) Teachers Evaluation in Transition: Emerging Roles and Evolving Methods. In Milman, Jason, and Darling Hammond, Linda, The New Handbook of Teacher Evaluation. California: Sage.

7. Ganihar N. Noorjehan. (2006) Performance Appraisal of Teachers. Neelkamal Publications Pvt. Ltd. Hyderabad.

8. Maurice E Troyer and Robert. C (1944) Evaluation in Education. Pace. American Council of education: Washington DC.

9. Venkataiah, N. (2011) Professional Development of Teachers. Neelkamal Publications Pvt. Ltd. Hyderabad.

❑❑❑❑

SUBJECT WISE INDEX

Appraisal

-      Potentialities: 62-63
-      Of teachers: 3-4, 7, 24
-      Teachers' opposition to: 2-3, 115-116
-      Procedures: 10-12, 25-28
-      Of appraisers: 13-14, 38
-      Steps for: 5, 10-12
-      Of senior subordinates: 126-127
-      In Education: 7-9, 20-22

Appraisal scale: 9
Accountability of the organisation: 38-39, 121
Apprentice training: 125
Annual Performance Appraisal: 39-41
Appraisal Skills: 41
Appraisal modus operandy: 43-44
Appraisal process: 61-64
Analytical review of self-appraisal: 72
Accountability centric appraisal: 77-78
Absence of timely feedback: 86, 162
Appraisal preparedness: 94
Appraisal interviews: 96-98
Appraisal report: 98-99
Appraisal discussion: 103-108
Bias: 85-86
Bottlenecks in appraisal: 109-121
Behaviour anchored Rating Scale: 136
Confidential reports: 1-3
Collaborative culture/teaching: 47-49
Critical analysis: 80-86
Central tendency: 84
Complaint redressal procedure: 99
Computerized rating scale: 133
Critical incident technique: 134

Contemplations on appraisal: 153-154
Continuous performance monitoring: 158-168
-       Advantages of Continuous Performance monitoring: 159
-       Disadvantages of: 159
Causes of skill deficiency: 161-162
Documentation: 40
Development centered: 49, 64
Diagnosis of appraisal errors: 86-87
Duties of appraiser: 151-152
Duties of managements: 148-150
Discrepancy statement: 160
Delight in poor performance: 163-164
Disinterest in good performance: 1664-165
Difference between educational and industrial appraisal: 20-22
Discussion/interview: 123
Evaluation: 1, 7, 24
Educational performance appraisal: 28
-       Principles of: 29
Effective integration: 55-57, 60-61
Employee centric appraisal: 80
Essay: 133-134
Effective appraisal: 154-155
-       Obstacles in: 110-116
Feedback: 7, 9, 10, 155
-       Effective: 155
-       Immediate 120
-       From students: 74-75
-       Significance of: 75-76
-       Expectations from: 76
Formative evaluation: 24
Formal performance appraisal: 39
Forced culture: 49-51
Forms of teacher appraisal: 76
Flattery: 81
Follow-up-actions: 99-102
Face to face: 105-106
Features of successful appraisal: 42-43
Facts based appraisal: 120
Forced distribution: 135

Forced choice: 135
Gains of appraisal: 47-48
General goals: 91-92
Graphic Rating Scale: 128-129
Good performance: 140-141
Halo error: 81
-       Drawbacks of halo error: 81
Hypocritical behaviour: 84
Human resource development: 122-141
Human resource planning: 138-140
Human resource department: 122-140
-       Duties of: 150
Hurdles in good performance: 164
Institutional goals: 24
Individual and organisational needs: 54-55
Incapabilities of appraisers: 86
Inspection: 96
Invisibility of educational results: 114
Introspection on educational goals: 117-118
Individualized instruction: 118
Inexperienced managers: 110-111
Information technology: 119-120
Incentives: 139
Incapable employees: 140
Irregular performance: 162
Judgmental: 65, 85
-       Features of: 65
Judgmental attitude: 88
Kinds of staff-appraisal: 63
Laissez fair: 65
-       Features of: 65
Leniency: 82-83
Lack of consensus: 113-114
Lack of interest: 163
Management: 9
-       Participative: 9, 26
Manpower planning: 10, 138-140
Measurement scales: 14
Managerial vision: 52-71

Mechanical theory: 58
Management centered: 64
Managerial goals: 91
Microteaching: 118
Management by objectives (MBO): 129-130
Motivation: 127, 139
Management's awakening: 142-157
Managerial roles: 148-149
Need based performance appraisal: 89-102
-       Goals of: 91-92
-       Procedures of: 92-93
New techniques and procedures: 118-119
Obscurity of educational effects: 111-113
Organisational management styles: 57
Organisational scenario and appraisal: 59-60
Organic theory: 58
Orientation: 124
On-job-training: 125-126
Off-job-training: 126
Performance appraisal: 1
-       Definitions of: 6
-       Philosophy of: 36-38
-       Principles of: 22-24, 93
-       Logic behind: 42-43, 148
-       Importance of: 3-4
-       Advantages of: 4-6, 137-138
-       Prerequisites of: 12-13
-       Procedure of: 10-12, 25-28, 70-88, 127-128
-       Guidelines for: 36-51
-       Goals: 5, 9, 11, 23-24, 37-38, 147
-       Preparation of: 14, 94-95
-       Procedure of: 127-128
-       Cycle of: 25-28
-       Systems of: 120
-       Tools of: 14-15, 27, 128
-       Review of: 39-40, 53
-       Onus of successful: 8, 13
-       Failures of successful: 44-46
-       In education: 7-8, 20-35

- Departmental: 9, 14-15
- Present scenario: 1
- Traditional techniques of: 1-3
- Drawbacks of: 3-4

Performance scale: 9
- Characteristics of: 11

Paired ranking: 135
Professional planning and development: 138-139
Professional development: 4, 9, 26-27, 64, 100-101, 122-127
Paired Comparison Tool: 130
Pre-appraisal discussion: 150
Policy statement: 43
Profession centric appraisal: 41, 78-79
Performance standards: 41-42, 149-150
Peer-appraisal: 95-96
Portfolio: 96
Problem solving: 106, 160
Prescriptive teaching: 118
Rapport: 44-47, 49-52
- Between teachers and management: 10, 12

Role play: 33-34
- Definition of: 33
- Qualities of: 34
- Features of: 34-35

Review of previous achievements: 39-40
Reflective perspective: 67-71
Reflective practitioner perspective: 69-71
Role of teachers: 114-115
- Responsibility of: 116, 147

Recent developments affecting education: 116-118
Rewards: 4, 10, 140
- Intrinsic reward: 141
- Extrinsic rewards: 140

Ranking: 134
Recruitments: 138
Root cause of discrepancy: 161
Self-appraisal: 4, 15-16, 27, 95
- Definitions of: 4, 15, 27
- Logic behind: 28-29

-         Advantages of: 28-29, 73
-         Procedures of: 31-33
-         Prior steps for: 73-74
Safety of records: 40-41
Subjectivity: 80-81
Skills: 9-10, 41
-         Definitions of: 10
-         Of pre-discussion: 107
-         Of main discussion: 107-108
Strictness: 83-84
Sense of humour: 73
Summative evaluation: 24
Seniors' appraisal: 43, 127
-         Components of: 43-45
Staff development review: 53-54
Student Rating Questionnaire: 68
Selection of appraisers: 94
Stimulants for appraisal discussion: 103-105
Standardized Appraisal Tools: 115
Staff differentiation: 118
Screening: 123
Structured interview: 123
Social Media Tools: 137
Screening Written Tests: 123
Selection: 123-124
Significance of discrepancy: 161
State of mind: 162-163
Teaching: 17
-         As an art: 2, 14, 29-30
Teachers' appraisers: 15-19
-         By students: 16-17
-         By parents: 17-18
-         By peers: 18-19
-         By management: 19
Three hundred sixty (360 degree) Tool: 75, 131-133
Technical perspective: 67-71
Tell and sell: 105
Tell and listen: 105-106
Team teaching: 118

Training: 125
Training system: 125
Training and development: 139
Unrealistic appraisal: 85
Unstructured interviews: 123
Vestibule training: 126
Voluntary co-operation: 47-49
Work standards: 134
Weighted Checklist: 135-136
X theory: 57
Y theory: 57-58

Thanks to

Arora Pankaj: 144
Arora Ashish: 75, 76
Bloom: 117
Burns & Stalker: 58
Bridges et al: 67, 69
Dennison and Shentor: 57
Elliot: 67, 69
Eraut: 69
Hargreaves: 45, 47
Ingversion and Chadbourne: 24
Kenneth Blanchard: 75
Kapagntala, Anjni Madhvi: 142
Katelyn Cavanaugh: 119
Mager: 117
Mohrman, Lawler and Resnick-West: 42
McGregor: 57
Piaget: 117
Rao, Kavita: 143
Ramsden: 68, 70
Robert Pace & Maurice Troyer: 7
Schon: 67
Scriven: 24
Sharma Sharad: 75
Subramanian, Raman: 75
Tomilson: 61

Table Index

Table 1: Collaborative versus Forced Culture

Table 2: Kinds of Pre-appraisal Discussions.

Table 3: Graphic Rating Scale.

Table 4 Three hundred sixty (360) degree Appraisal Matrix.

❑❑❑❑